Series/Number 07-116

D1239777

MONTE CARLO SIMULATION

CHRISTOPHER Z. MOONEY
West Virginia University

SAGE PUBLICATIONS
International Educational and Professional Publisher
Thousand Oaks   London   New Delhi

For information address:

SAGE Publications, Inc.
2455 Teller Road
Thousand Oaks, California 91320
E-mail: order@sagepub.com

SAGE Publications Ltd.
6 Bonhill Street
London EC2A 4PU
United Kingdom

SAGE Publications India Pvt. Ltd.
M-32 Market
Greater Kailash I
New Delhi 110 048 India

Printed in the United States of America

Library of Congress Cataloging-in-Publication Data

Mooney, Christopher Z.
    Monte Carlo simulation / author, Christopher Z. Mooney.
        p.   cm. — (Quantitative applications in the social sciences ;
    Vol. #116)
    Includes bibliographical references (p.   ).
    ISBN 0-8039-5943-5 (pbk.)
        1.   Monte Carlo method.   I. Title.   II. Series: Sage university
    papers series.   Quantitative applications in the social sciences ;
    no.   116.
    QA298.M66   1997
    519.2'82—dc21
                                                                        96-45873
                                                                        CIP
97   98   99   00   01   02   03   10   9   8   7   6   5   4   3   2   1

Acquiring Editor:	C. Deborah Laughton
Editorial Assistant:	Eileen Carr
Production Editor:	Sherrise M. Purdum
Production Assistant:	Denise Santoyo
Typesetter/Designer:	Andrea D. Swanson

When citing a university paper, please use the proper form. Remember to cite the current Sage University Paper series title and include the paper number. One of the following formats can be adapted (depending on the style manual used):

(1) Mooney, C. Z. (1997) *Monte Carlo Simulation.* Sage University Paper series on Quantitative Applications in the Social Sciences, 07-116. Thousand Oaks, CA: Sage.
OR
(2) Mooney, C. Z. (1997) *Monte Carlo Simulation* (Sage University Paper series on Quantitative Applications in the Social Sciences, series no. 07-116). Thousand Oaks, CA: Sage.

CONTENTS

ACKNOWLEDGMENTS

This monograph began as a section of my notes for the course in nonparametric inference I teach at the European Consortium for Social Research's Essex Summer School in Data Analysis and Collection. I thank Eric Tanenbaum, the director of the Summer School, for supporting this course, and I thank my students for their input. I also thank Bob Duval, Gary King, Hugh Ward, Bruce Worton, and an anonymous reviewer for reading the entire manuscript in an earlier version and offering important suggestions, Neal Beck and Jonathan Katz for the use of their published Monte Carlo simulation results, Burak Saltoglu for his research assistance in an early phase of this project, the British Academy for financial support, and Aptech Systems for a review copy of GAUSS. This monograph is dedicated to Laura, Allison, and Charlie, who are my constant reminders that real life is better than simulation.

SERIES EDITOR'S INTRODUCTION

The statistics of classical parametric inference inform us about how the world works to the extent necessary assumptions are met. In regression analysis on a set of social observations, suppose the slope of X is statistically significant and BLUE (best linear unbiased estimator). Then we have a clear expectation for what actually happens to the dependent variable Y when X changes one unit. But what if the usual conditions for inference are not met? Perhaps, to name some possibilities, the error term is heteroskedastic, correlated with the independent variable, or skewed. Given any of those, we know that our inferences from ordinary least squares (OLS) risk being seriously off the mark. The calculations we run would become little more than exercises for the imagination.

When certain regression assumptions are violated or are under suspicion of violation, Monte Carlo simulation can be a way out. For example, it allows exploration of parameter estimation granting a variety of distributions—uniform, Pareto, exponential, normal, lognormal, chi-square, Student's t, mixture, or beta. Besides providing a check on single-equation OLS results, Monte Carlo simulation has been used to compare estimator properties from multiequation systems, for example, two-stage versus three-stage estimators. Furthermore, it promises considerable payoff in the study of valuable statistics that are simply calculated but about which little is known inferentially, for example, the median or the absolute average deviation.

In addition to the benefits of a Monte Carlo simulation, Professor Mooney explains its logic. The population of interest is simulated. From the *pseudo-population*, repeated random samples are drawn. The statistic under study is computed in each *pseudo-sample*, and its sampling distribution is examined for insights into its behavior. Although the logic is not hard to grasp, the execution can be. Here the author makes a major contribution, for he reports in careful detail how to prepare the computer algorithm. His explication of the GAUSS code has special worth given that standard statistical packages do not contain a Monte Carlo option. Fortunately, the discussion uses several research examples. In one, a political viii

scientist, concerned about the quality of OLS estimates from real data, simulates the attitude of legislators toward government regulation of business. In another, an index of corporatism undergoes investigation through simulation.

Monte Carlo work is highly computer intensive, and complicated models can consume large amounts of time, even requiring days on a mainframe. Besides model complexity, this is due partly to the number of trials. Nowadays, simulations of 25,000 trials often are run. Mooney recognizes that, in this enterprise, errors can occur and can be costly. Wisely, he counsels the researcher to comprend the social process under investigation, work carefully piece by piece, and check regularly for mistakes. Although we always should heed such advice, it is doubly important for innovative investigations on the statistical frontier.

—*Michael S. Lewis-Beck*
Series Editor

MONTE CARLO SIMULATION

CHRISTOPHER Z. MOONEY
West Virginia University

1. INTRODUCTION

Social scientists use statistical analysis to describe and make inferences regarding social phenomena using measured variables. The idea is to estimate a social characteristic, θ, with an estimator, $\hat{\theta}$, computed from observed data. The specific mathematical manipulations to which we subject our data have been developed largely through the use of analytic mathematics so that the resulting estimators meet important and intuitive criteria—unbiasedness, efficiency, and consistency. For example, going back to Gauss and Laplace, there is good theoretical reason to believe that if we add up the values of an observed variable, x, on n cases chosen from a population at random and divide by n, then we will get a good estimate of the central tendency of that variable in that population, the statistical behavior of which is well understood.

However, most of this mathematical theory is conditional. For example, as most second-year social science graduate students know, for ordinary least squares (OLS) estimates of regression slopes to be unbiased and efficient, a number of conditions regarding the population relationship must hold true. If these conditions do not hold, then analytical mathematics provides no information about the properties and behavior of these statistics in random samples. Furthermore, there are many potentially useful statistics for which these mathematics have not yet been worked out, if indeed they ever can be. For example, how does the difference in sample medians behave in random samples (e.g., Groseclose, 1994)? Is it unbiased? Is it consistent? These open questions make the use of this statistic, along with a host of others being developed continuously, impractical for the social scientist relying solely on analytical mathematics for his or her understanding of the estimator.

At the center of the evaluation of the behavior of a statistic is its *sampling distribution*, that is, the range of values the statistic can take on in a random sample from a given population and the probabilities associated with those values (Mohr, 1990, pp. 18-19). A statistic's bias can be assessed by

1

examining the expected value of its sampling distribution, and its variability and functional form allow for an assessment of the statistic's efficiency and are vital to making inferences to the population parameter. The analytical evaluation of a statistic is based on the theoretical development of its sampling distribution. But what can a social scientist do either when the conditions necessary for the mathematical theory to be valid do not hold or when there is no strong theory regarding the statistic he or she wants to use?

Monte Carlo simulation offers an alternative to analytical mathematics for understanding a statistic's sampling distribution and evaluating its behavior in random samples. Monte Carlo simulation does this empirically using *random samples from known populations of simulated data* to track a statistic's behavior. The basic concept is straightforward: If a statistic's sampling distribution is the density function of the values it could take on in a given population, then its estimate is the relative frequency distribution of the values of that statistic that were *actually observed* in many samples drawn from that population. Because it usually is impractical for social scientists to sample actual data multiple times, we use artificially generated data that resemble the real thing in relevant ways. The recent availability of high-speed computers makes this approach now widely practical for the first time in history.

Consider estimating the regression slope for a bivariate model in which the error term is correlated with the independent variable and highly skewed and the sample size is 20. In this situation, the behavior of the OLS estimate of the slope is unknown, as neither the Gauss-Markov theorem nor the central limit theorem (the bases of the analytical assessment of OLS slope coefficients) applies. But by simulating this situation using artificial data, estimating the OLS slope multiple times, and constructing the relative frequency distribution of those estimates, we can gain an understanding of the behavior of this statistic in this situation. Figure 1.1 displays such a relative frequency distribution. The *true* value of the slope (as defined in the computer generating algorithm discussed in Chapter 2) is 2.0. But note that the distribution of these 1,000 slope estimates is centered at around 12.0, indicating a severe upward bias in the OLS estimate. Furthermore, a Jarque-Bera test for normality indicates that this distribution is not normally distributed but rather some what leptokurtic (i.e., more peaked than a normal distribution). These facts had to be divined through the use of a simple Monte Carlo simulation because the traditional analytical mathematics for OLS slopes could not be applied legitimately. Had I assumed that the traditional analytics of the Gauss-Markov theorem were applicable

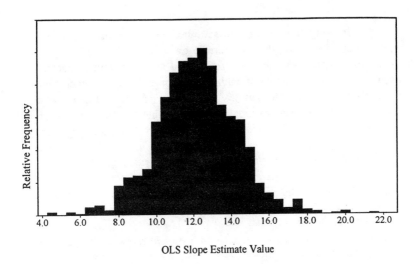

Figure 1.1. Relative Frequency Distribution of Ordinary Least Squares Slope Estimate, Given Model Specifications in Text

here (certainly not an unheard of occurrence in the social sciences), the conclusions I would have come to regarding the social phenomenon in question would have been severely compromised.

The Monte Carlo estimate of a statistic's sampling distribution can be used in a variety of ways to understand statistical and social processes. Some of the uses of Monte Carlo simulation to be examined in more detail in Chapter 4 include the following:

— conducting inference using statistics with only weak mathematical theory,
— testing null hypotheses under a variety of plausible conditions,
— assessing the robustness of parametric inference to violations of its assumptions,
— assessing the quality of inferential methods, and
— comparing the properties of two or more estimators.

1.1 The Monte Carlo Principle

The principle behind Monte Carlo simulation is that the behavior of a statistic in random samples can be assessed by the empirical process of actually drawing lots of random samples and *observing* this behavior. The strategy for doing this is to create an artificial "world," or *pseudo-population*, which resembles the real world in all relevant respects. This pseudo-population consists of mathematical procedures for generating sets of numbers that resemble samples of data drawn from the true population. We then use this pseudo-population to conduct multiple trials of the statistical procedure of interest to investigate how that procedure behaves across samples.

The basic Monte Carlo procedure is as follows:

1. Specify the pseudo-population in symbolic terms in such a way that it can be used to generate samples. This usually means developing a computer algorithm to generate data in a specified manner.
2. Sample from the pseudo-population (a *pseudo-sample*) in ways reflective of the statistical situation of interest, for example, with the same sampling strategy, sample size, and so forth.
3. Calculate $\hat{\theta}$ in the pseudo-sample and store it in a vector, $\hat{\theta}$.
4. Repeat Steps 2 and 3 t times, where t is the number of *trials*.
5. Construct a relative frequency distribution of the resulting $\hat{\theta}_t$ values, which is the Monte Carlo estimate of the sampling distribution of $\hat{\theta}$ under the conditions specified by the pseudo-population and the sampling procedures.

Clearly, Monte Carlo simulation is very simple in concept as it flows naturally from the conception of what a sampling distribution is. The complicated aspects of the technique are (a) writing the computer code to simulate the data conditions desired and (b) interpreting the estimated sampling distribution. This monograph explains these to convey a practical understanding of how one undertakes this procedure and uses the results.

When describing any procedure in the following chapters, I provide a set of intuitive algorithm steps and specific GAUSS code to execute it. GAUSS is a highly flexible, matrix algebra-based, medium-level computer language in wide use in the social sciences, particularly among economists (Aptech Systems, 1994). It is fast and efficient, and this is vital in conducting Monte Carlo experiments in which thousands or millions of calculations are executed. Given the paucity of preprogrammed Monte Carlo simulation procedures in the more commonly used software packages (e.g., SAS, SPSS),[1] if one is to conduct Monte Carlo simulation, then a fast and programmable package such as GAUSS is necessary. The GAUSS language also is relatively intuitive, and the translation of its commands into another language with which the reader is more familiar should not be difficult. In GAUSS, comments are bracketed by /* and */ signs, as seen throughout the text, and the actual GAUSS commands are printed in the text in a contrasting font. All GAUSS code in this monograph is available on the World Wide Web at http://www.polsci.wvu.edu/faculty/mooney/mc.htm.

2. GENERATING INDIVIDUAL SAMPLES FROM A PSEUDO-POPULATION

The first step in conducting a Monte Carlo simulation experiment is to define the pseudo-population. The researcher must carefully specify those components of the pseudo-population that are deterministic and those that are stochastic, the forms and values that each of these components takes, and the components that are to be held constant across experiments and those that are to be varied. All of these considerations should be based on substantive theory, although practical and experimental design considerations will play a role.

2.1 Setting Up a Population Generating Computer Algorithm

In most Monte Carlo simulation experiments, the researcher defines the pseudo-population as a computer algorithm that generates artificial data in a way that simulates how the social process under consideration generates data in the real world. The pseudo-population therefore is not physically observed but rather represented by the set of computer commands used to generate the data. The researcher then can use his or her knowledge of this pseudo-population to understand better the behavior of the statistical estimates derived from real data.

These computer algorithms will produce three types of data: constants, deterministic variables, and random variables. Because the random component of most social processes is what makes statistical estimation problematic, and because random variables are the most complex and difficult to generate, it is the last of these three types of data that I consider at greatest length.

Consider a simple regression model as the symbolic representation of a theory about the relationship between two variables, X and Y:

$$Y_i = \beta_1 + \beta_2 X_i + \varepsilon_i. \tag{2.1}$$

In keeping with the standard notation with which most social scientists are familiar, in this model there are two constants (β_1 and β_2) that represent the parameters of the model, one deterministic variable (X) that varies in a specified and systematic manner as in a classic experiment, and two random variables (ε and Y). To generate data from this model (e.g., to compare various estimators of the parameters), computer commands need to be written to define each of these components.

Constants are straightforward to define. One merely selects some scalar values that seem reasonable based on substantive theory, previous research, and the specific tests to be undertaken with the simulation. For example, empirical work in this area might suggest $\beta_1 = 2.0$ and $\beta_2 = 1.0$. Once a value for a constant has been determined, it is a simple matter to define that value in most programming languages. GAUSS code to do this is

```
b1 = 2.0;      /*set b1 to 2.0*/
b2 = 1.0;      /*set b2 to 1.0*/
```

Some constants are not as easy to set as those in this regression model. For example, setting the correlation matrix for a set of variables is more complex (see Section 2.3.2.1).

Deterministic variables are vectors of numbers that take on a range of values in a prespecified, nonrandom manner. For example, in a classic regression model, the values of the independent variables are fixed by the experimenter. The easiest way in which to generate such a vector of numbers is to do so sequentially. That is, start on a given number and add a constant to it repeatedly until the desired number of cases has been generated. The GAUSS code to do this is

```
x = seqa(0,2,20);      /*start at 0 and progress by 2's with a
                         total of 20 cases*/.
```

Here x would be the set $\{0, 2, 4, \ldots 38\}$. Alternatively, a variable can be generated in multiplicative sequence in GAUSS:

```
x = seqm(2,3,10);      /* start at 2 and increase by factors of 3
                         with a total of 10 cases*/
```

The variable in this case would be the set $\{2, 6, 18, \ldots, 39366\}$. Because multiplicative sequences increase so quickly, factors of between −2 and 2 typically are used.

A final type of deterministic variable probably should not be called a "variable" at all because it does not vary across cases. Sometimes it is necessary to generate a vector of the same number, for example, as for the constant column in an **X** matrix for a regression problem. This is done in GAUSS by multiplying an $(n \times 1)$ column of ones by the desired value:

```
x = ones(n,1);      /*set x as an (n × 1) matrix of ones*/
x = x * 56.7;       /*multiply x by 56.7, yielding an (n × 1)
                      vector of the number 56.7*/
```

2.2 Generating Single Random Variables

We can now write a computer program that defines all of the components of Equation 2.1 except the random variables, Y and ε. Furthermore, Y can be generated as a function of the components on the right-hand side of the equation. Therefore, all that remains to be defined is ε. But it is the generation of ε, and the generation of random variables generally, that is most difficult in a Monte Carlo experiment, for two reasons. First, it often is very difficult to determine how a variable is distributed in the real world and which of the many standard distributions best represents it. Second, the computer algorithms to generate random variables are a good deal more complex than those needed to generate constants and deterministic variables.

More important, the proper generation of random variables is critical to the success of a Monte Carlo simulation. This is because the random component of a statistical model is largely what drives the sampling distribution of $\hat{\theta}$. For example, in small samples, an OLS slope estimate will have a different sampling distribution if the error term is normally distributed rather than highly skewed (Ghurye, 1949). For this reason, most classical parametric (and even many nonparametric) inference techniques rely heavily on assumptions about the shape of the model's random component.

Because of the importance and difficulty of generating random variables properly, I devote considerable space to this topic. But prior to describing the generation of a variety of types of random variables, it will be useful to review a bit of probability theory with respect to random variables.

A random variable is the realization of some event that can take on a range of values, with the probability of each of these values occurring being determined by the variable's *distribution function*, F(X). F(X) is the function such that when a value for X, say x, is plugged into it, the probability is returned that a random case from a variable with that distribution function would have a value less than x. For example, the distribution function for a standard normal variable is

$$F(x) = \Pr(X \leq x) = (\sqrt{2\pi})^{-1} \int_{-\infty}^{x} e^{-\frac{1}{2}x^2} dx. \tag{2.2}$$

If you plugged the value $x = 1.96$ into the right-hand side of this equation, the result would be $\Pr(X \leq x) = .975$. Theoretically there is an infinite number of distribution functions at work in the world, but in practice a relatively small number have been formalized and used in modeling statistical processes.

Once a variable is defined in terms of its distribution function, a variety of other useful attributes of that variable are determined. For a continuous random variable, the *probability density function* (PDF), $f(x)$, is the function that maps the probability of x falling *between* two values of X. A graphic display of the PDF is particularly useful in visualizing a variable's distributional form, as it is analogous to a histogram for a discrete variable. The familiar image of the normal distribution as a "bell-shaped curve" is derived from viewing its PDF. The *inverse distribution function*, $G(\alpha)$, is the function such that if we plug in a *probability value*, α, it will yield the value of x such that $\Pr(X \leq x) = \alpha$. Thus it is the inverse of the distribution function. The $G(\alpha)$ is particularly useful in generating certain random variates, as will be discussed.

Distributions that have the same general function but differ in their parameter values are known as *distribution families*. For example, a variable that is normally distributed with a mean of 32.3 and a standard deviation of 47.8 clearly is different from a variable that is normally distributed with a mean of 2.3 and a standard deviation of 0.57. But just as clearly, the two are in the same general family of distributions and have far more in common with one another statistically than either would have with a lognormally distributed variable with the same mean and standard deviation. This raises the issue of *parameters* in distribution functions. Most general distribution functions include a small number of constants that determine the member of the distribution family being specified. A parameter will determine the location, scale, and/or shape of the specified distribution (Evans, Hastings, & Peacock, 1993, p. 21).

Each distribution function also has its characteristic *range* of permissible values of X. For some distributions this range is infinite (e.g., the normal distribution), for some it is truncated in one direction (e.g., the exponential distribution), and for some it is truncated at both ends (e.g., the uniform distribution).

Finally, the *mean*, *variance*, *skewness*, and *kurtosis* of a distribution function often are important in Monte Carlo work. The mean and variance are of special interest in that it usually is the case that different distributions, even those in the same family, will not have the same values for these. This can cause difficulty when comparing Monte Carlo experiments with random variables drawn from different functions. Therefore, it usually is good practice to *standardize* generated variables with respect to mean and variance by subtracting from each case the *theoretical* mean of the generating distribution and dividing by the square root of the *theoretical* variance. The skewness and kurtosis of a distribution describe the type and degree of nonnormality, which often is of interest in statistical analysis.

One of the key problems in conducting Monte Carlo simulation is determining which distribution function a random variable in the pseudo-population should assume. There are many distributions from which to choose, and there often is little practical or even theoretical guidance as to which distribution to use in a particular experiment (Johnson, 1987, pp. 2-3). When selecting a distribution function to generate a random variable in a Monte Carlo simulation, the researcher must consider at least three aspects of the problem. In each of these considerations, the researcher needs to keep closely in mind the types of variables and processes being simulated and the design of the experiments being undertaken. First, will the *range* of the data desired be delivered by this function? Second, does the *shape* of the distribution resemble the shape required? The PDF is particularly useful here to give a feel for the fit between simulated and real data. Specific goodness-of-fit tests sometimes can be used to test this congruity (Ross, 1990, pp. 148-156). Third, does the distribution function allow for the ready *variation* of the aspects of the distribution that the researcher wants to explore across experiments? For example, when examining the effect of nonnormality on parametric inference, it is helpful to use a family of distributions that can move smoothly away from normality simply by adjusting the parameters of the function.

In the following sections, I describe and show how to generate variables from a variety of distribution functions with an eye toward their usefulness in Monte Carlo simulation. This means, first, that they all can be generated easily and efficiently in a computer program. But just as important, these distributions have a special position in statistical theory (e.g., the normal distribution), have been observed to resemble data of interest to social scientists (e.g., the Pareto distribution), and/or allow for ready variation of important aspects of a variable's distribution such as its skewness or kurtosis (e.g., the chi-square

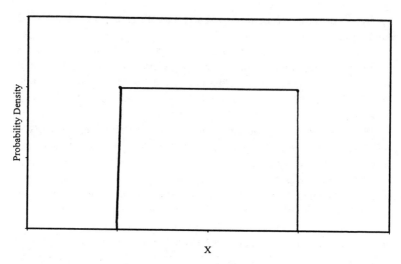

Figure 2.1. Probability Density Function of U(*a*, *b*)

distribution). Many other well-studied distributions exist and can be examined in the standard references on the subject (e.g., Evans et al., 1993; Johnson & Kotz, 1970a, 1970b; Johnson, Kotz, & Kemp, 1992).

2.2.1 Continuous Distribution Functions

A continuous distribution function is one that can deliver any value of *x* that lies within its range. The continuous distributions discussed here are the uniform, Pareto, exponential, normal, lognormal, chi-square, Student's *t*, mixture, and beta distributions.

2.2.1.1 The Uniform Distribution: U(*a*, *b*)

A random variable with a uniform distribution, U(*a*, *b*), can take on any value in its range with equal probability, where the parameters *a* and *b* are the lower and upper bounds of this range. The PDF (Figure 2.1) shows the characteristic plateau of a U(*a*, *b*) variable. It is a symmetric, platykurtic (flatter than a normal distribution) distribution. Note that neither skew nor kurtosis is affected by the parameters (Table 2.1).

In its standard form, U(0, 1), the uniform distribution is the building block of all Monte Carlo simulation work in that from it, in one way or

TABLE 2.1
Characteristics of the Uniform, Pareto,
Exponential, and Normal Distributions

	Uniform	*Pareto*	*Exponential*	*Normal*
Notation	$U(a, b)$	$Par(a, c)$	$Exp(a, b)$	$N(a, b)$
Parameters	a = lower limit; b = upper limit	a = mode and lower limit; $(a > 0)$ $c > 0$	a = lower limit; $b > 0$	a = mean; b = variance $(b > 0)$
Distribution function	$F(x) = (x - a)/(b - a)$	$F(x) = 1 - (a/x)^c$	$F(x) = 1 - \exp[-(x - a)/b]$	$F(x) = (\sqrt{2\pi b})^{-1} \int_{-\infty}^{x} e^{\frac{-(x-a)^2}{2b}} dx$
Probability density function	$f(x) = 1/(b - a)$	$f(x) = c*a^c/x^{c+1}$	$f(x) = (1/b)*\exp[-(x - a)/b]$	$f(x) = (\sqrt{2\pi b})^{-1} e^{\frac{-(x-a)^2}{2b}}$
Inverse distribution function	$G(\alpha) = a + \alpha(b - a)$	$G(\alpha) = a(1 - \alpha)^{-1/c}$	$G(\alpha) = a - [b*\ln(1 - \alpha)]$	—
Range	$a \leq x \leq b$	$a \leq x < \infty$	$a \leq x < \infty$	$-\infty < x < \infty$
Mean	$(a + b)/2$	$c*a/(c - 1)$, if $c > 1$	$b + a$	a
Variance	$(b - a)^2/12$	$c*a^2/[(c - 1)^2 (c - 2)]$ if $c > 2$	b^2	b
Skew	0	—	2	0
Kurtosis	9/5	—	9	3

another, variables with all other distribution functions are derived. This is because the U(0, 1) distribution, with its $0 \leq x \leq 1$ range, can be used to simulate a set of random probabilities, which are used to generate other distribution functions through the inverse transformation and acceptance-rejection methods.

To simulate a uniform distribution, we need to be able to generate a set of numbers that are equiprobable, independent, and (ideally) reproducible.

The first two criteria are theoretical requirements, and the latter criterion is practical in that it is important to be able to replicate results as a check on the simulation program. Mechanical methods have been used since prehistoric times to generate equiprobable outcomes. Drawing balls from urns, drawing lots from hats, and flipping coins have been used for a variety of purposes, from choosing political leaders in ancient Greece to settling ties on draft picks for the National Basketball Association. With a well-mixed set of balls, chips, or slips of paper, this indeed is an ideal way of selecting truly uniformly and independently distributed random numbers. But this method is time consuming, open to faults caused by human fatigue, and (most important) not reproducible. An alternative is the use of a commercially assembled random number table (RAND Corporation, 1955). If these numbers are fed into a computer, then independent and equiprobable random numbers can be drawn automatically. Although this method certainly is quicker and more reliable than drawing numbers out of a hat, it still can be rather slow and runs the risk of exhausting the table if many simulations are conducted.

Given the drawbacks of truly independent uniform numbers, techniques have been developed for generating numbers through algebraic algorithms that can be held to have the *characteristics* of such numbers. Numbers generated in such a fashion are said to be *pseudo-random* but can be used in place of random numbers within certain limits if they pass rigorous tests for uniformity and independence (Rubinstein, 1981, pp. 26-33). The key advantages of this approach are that, first, because the algorithm is at root deterministic, the same series of numbers can be reproduced and, second, they tend to be very fast. The problem with pseudo-random numbers is that they begin to repeat after time. However, the length of the series of numbers that most pseudo-random number generators in use today will yield before repeating—that is, their "period"—is on the order of hundreds of millions or billions. Within these limits, pseudo-random numbers can be used quite adequately in simulation studies. For economy, henceforth I simply use the term *random numbers* to refer to pseudo-random numbers.

The most commonly used algorithms for generating random numbers from a U(0, 1) distribution are called multiple congruential methods and proceed as follows (Ross, 1990, pp. 36-38):

1. Select a and m, positive integers, and x_{seed} as a starting point for the series.
2. Calculate $x_n = a*x_{n-1}$ modulo m, using x_{seed} as the first x_{n-1}.
3. Repeat Step 2 until the desired number of cases of x have been generated.

In Step 2, *modulo* means to divide the product $(a*x_{n-1})$ by m and keep the remainder as x_n. This process yields a series of numbers that act like independent random numbers distributed as U(0, 1) with a period of m (unless the same number happens to come up twice as x_n). Selecting the proper value for a and m has been studied extensively (MacLaren & Marsaglia, 1965), but for a 32-bit machine $m = 2^{31} - 1$ and $a = 7^5$ perform well (Ross, 1990, p. 37). With an m of this magnitude, the procedure will have a very long period and, except in cases of extremely large and complex simulations, numbers resulting from such a procedure will act randomly.[2]

Most computer packages have built-in a random number generator that will produce a U(0, 1) variable with a single command. Although the defaults for m and a generally are fine for most purposes, the researcher always should set the seed manually to allow for replication. Once the seed is set, random numbers will be generated continually from the last x_n obtained, even if it was for a procedure farther back in the program. Therefore, if a program has millions of random numbers to be generated (e.g., a multiexperiment Monte Carlo simulation of bootstrapping with a large sample size), then reseeding occasionally within the program will avoid a problem with periodicity.

GAUSS uses the multiple congruential method and allows the programmer to set m, a, and the seed. The defaults are $m = 2^{31} - 1$ and $a = 397,204,094$, and the seed is set by the internal clock. The following commands yield an x distributed U(0, 1) with the seed being set by the researcher:

```
rndseed 47;                 /*set the seed for the random
                            number generator to 47*/
x = rndu(n,c);              /*set x to be an (n × c) matrix of
                            U(0, 1) numbers*/.
```

To transform a U(0, 1) variable into a U(a, b) variable, one first multiplies the U(0, 1) variable by the absolute range desired. For example, multiplying a U(0, 1) variable by 3 will yield a new variable with a range of 0 to 3. To shift the position of this distribution on the number line, one then adds the lower bound, a, to the new variable. In this example, after the absolute range has been set to 3, adding 5 to each case of the variable will set its range as 5 to 8. In GAUSS, this is done as follows if $x \sim$ U(0, 1):

```
x = (x * (b-a)) + a;        /*set x to be distributed as U(a, b)*/.
```

14

2.2.1.2 The Inverse Transformation Method

The inverse transformation method of generating random variables follows directly from the insight that the inverse distribution function, $G(\alpha)$, yields the value of x such that $\Pr(X \leq x) = \alpha$ for X distributed as $F(X)$. If we can generate a vector of random probabilities and feed them into $G(\alpha)$, then the output will be a vector of random numbers distributed as $F(X)$. Given the discussion in the previous section, it is a simple matter to generate a U(0, 1) variable that acts like a vector of random probabilities. The issue is to specify $G(\alpha)$ for a given distribution. Although $G(\alpha)$ does not exist in closed form for all distribution functions, when it does exist a random variable can be efficiently generated using this method (Rubinstein, 1981, p. 41).[3] In this section, I discuss two continuous functions that can be used to generate variables with this approach: the Pareto and exponential distributions. Other continuous functions that can be simulated by the inverse transformation method include the Cauchy, Wiebull, Gumbel, logistic, power function, and Rayleigh distributions.

2.2.1.2.1 The Pareto Distribution: Par(a, c)

The Pareto distribution was first formulated by the 19th-century economist of the same name as an approximation for the distribution of income in a society. It is left truncated at its first parameter, a, and its PDF is a curve sloping downward to the right with a long tail (Figure 2.2). Its other parameter, c, defines the steepness of the descent of the function and is the y-axis intercept. As c increases above 2, the descent is very steep indeed and the distribution is in fact unstable and seldom used (Evans et al., 1993, p. 119). To generate a left-skewed, Pareto-shaped variable, multiply a Pareto distributed variable by -1.

Although there has been much debate as to the precision with which this function actually fits the distribution of income (Johnson & Kotz, 1970a, p. 233), it has been used as an approximation for a wide variety of other phenomena including the size of U.S. cities, the number of slaves per owner in the old U.S. South, landholdings in Norman England, frequencies of words in some native North American languages, and even the intervals between patterns of notes in a Mozart bassoon concerto (Badger, 1980; Crowell, 1977, pp. 88-98)! Therefore, the Pareto distribution is useful in simulating these sorts of social variables.

The generation of a Par(a, c) distributed variable follows the general approach of inverse transformation, using $G(\alpha)$ from Table 2.1. First,

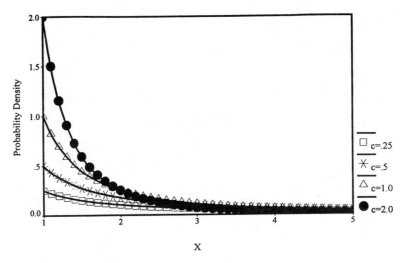

Figure 2.2. Probability Density Functions of Par(1, *c*)

generate a variable, *y* ~ U(0, 1), with the desired number of cases to serve as a vector of random probabilities. Second, set the parameter values as desired. Third, feed *y* into the inverse distribution function as α to yield *x* distributed in the manner specified. In GAUSS, the generation of a Par(*a*, *c*) distributed variable, *x*, would proceed as follows:

```
y = rndu(n,1);              /*set y as an (n × 1) vector
                            distributed as U(0, 1)@*/
a = 1; c = 2;               /*set a and c parameters to
                            equal 1 and 2, respectively*/
x = a * ((1-y)^(-1/c));     /*yield x distributed as Par(1, 2)*/
```

2.2.1.2.2 The Exponential Distribution: Exp(*a*, *b*)

The exponential distribution is another family of right-skewed distributions, but with different properties and uses than those of the Pareto. It is truncated at the parameter, *a*, and its dispersion is controlled by the parameter, *b*, which is the inverse of the *y* intercept (Figure 2.3). The standard deviation of the distribution is *b*, and the mean is *a* + *b*. The skew and kurtosis are constant at 2 and 9, respectively, regardless of the parameter values (Table 2.1).

16

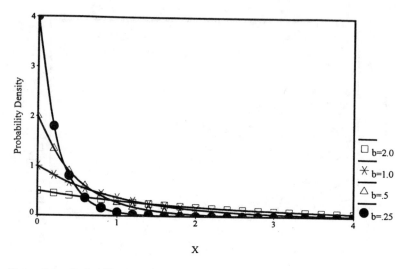

Figure 2.3. Probability Density Functions of Exp(0, *b*)

The exponential distribution has been found to mimic a variable of importance to medical researchers and industrial engineers, among others: the life span of an item or a person (Johnson & Kotz, 1970a, p. 208). That is, the time that a person is expected to live from any point onward is exponentially distributed. A unique attribute of the exponential distribution is that it is "memoryless," meaning that its shape is the same from any starting point moving to the right as it is from any other starting point (Ross, 1990, pp. 25-26). Therefore, the probability distribution of the time a car will survive past its first year is the same shape as that for its survival past its 10th year.

To generate a variable distributed as Exp(*a*, *b*) in GAUSS, follow the inverse transformation method[4]:

```
y = rndu(n,1);              /*set y as an (n × 1) vector
                            distributed as U(0, 1)*/
a = 1; b = 2;               /*set a and b parameters to equal 1
                            and 2, respectively*/
x = a-(b * (ln(y)));        /*yield x distributed as Exp(1, 2)*/
```

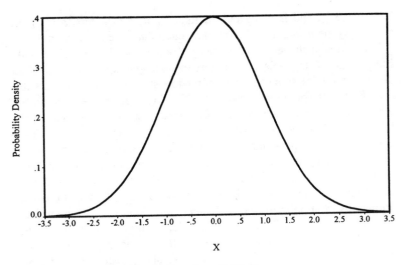

Figure 2.4. Probability Density Function of N(0, 1)

2.2.1.3 The Composition Method

The composition method is an alternative to the inverse transformation method to be used when the inverse distribution function cannot be derived or when it is complex and takes a long time to compute (Johnson, 1987, pp. 19-23). This method involves generating one or more variables from some other distribution (e.g., via the inverse transformation method) and then combining and transforming this (these) variable(s) in such a way that results in a variable with the desired distribution.[5] Here I discuss the generation of the normal, lognormal, chi-square, Student's t, and mixture distributions. Other continuous distributions that can be generated with the composition method include the Cauchy, Erlang, F, Laplace, and triangular distributions.

2.2.1.3.1 The Normal Distribution: N(a, b)

Undoubtedly the most widely studied and familiar statistical distribution is the normal, or Gaussian, distribution. Its PDF is as familiar to the social scientist as the periodic table is to the chemist (Table 2.1 and Figure 2.4). It is a symmetric bell-shaped curve, with a constant skewness (0.0) and kurtosis (3.0), and is characterized fully by its parameters, a (or more commonly the mean, μ) and b (or more commonly the variance, σ^2).

The normal distribution was developed and studied by the earliest of the Enlightenment statisticians due to its excellent approximations both of the distribution of the sum of a series of random shocks and of other distributions such as the binomial (Plackett, 1958). An important use of the normal distribution in simulation studies is as the baseline for checking parametric inference techniques given that from Gauss to Fisher, statisticians developed the bulk of parametric inference theory based on assumptions of normality (Plackett, 1972). It is good practice when evaluating the impact of a model assumption violation to check the simulation results for a pseudo-population for which the assumption holds true. Another use of the normal distribution in Monte Carlo simulation is in simulating attributes that take on this distribution. For example, intelligence and body weight and height in a given gender are distributed at least approximately normally. Finally, the normal distribution is useful in generating several other distributions via the composition method, as discussed in the following.

Unfortunately, the inverse distribution function of the normal distribution is intractable, and there is not a simple composition method for it. But because the normal distribution is so widely used, most computer packages provide a procedure to generate a standard normal variable, N(0, 1).[6] An N(0, 1) variable can be transformed into an N(a, b) variable by multiplying it by $\sqrt{b}$ and adding a. In GAUSS,

```
y = rndn(n,1);              /*set y as an (n × 1) vector
                              distributed as N(0, 1)*/
a = 1; b = 2;               /*set a and b parameters to equal
                              1 and 2, respectively*/
x = a + (sqrt(b) * y);      /*yield x distributed as N(1, 2)*/
```

2.2.1.3.2 The Lognormal Distribution: L(a, b)

Exponentiating a normally distributed variable yields a lognormally distributed one, a right-skewed variable found to be useful in describing a range of economic, social, and biological phenomena (e.g., Gaddum, 1945). Many of these phenomena have also been suggested to take on a Pareto distribution, but there is a clear difference between the Pareto and the lognormal to the left of the mode (Figures 2.2 and 2.5). There is evidence that although the Pareto distribution describes the skewed social

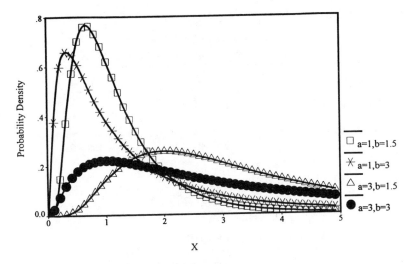

Figure 2.5. Probability Density Functions of L(a, b)

phenomena discussed in Section 2.2.1.2.1 better in the extreme right tail, the lognormal may describe them better in the main portion of the range (Fisk, 1961). Therefore, the choice between these two for a researcher trying to simulate such a variable will likely depend on which portion of the distribution is important in the experiment.

The two parameters of an L(a, b) distribution are derived from the parent normal distribution's mean and variance, where $a = \exp(\mu)$ and $b = \exp(\sigma^2)$. The parameter a is the median of the distribution, and the skewness and kurtosis vary with the b parameter (Table 2.2). Unlike the Pareto distribution, the range of the L(a, b) always is left truncated at 0.[7]

The GAUSS commands to generate an L(a, b) variable are

```
y = rndn(n,1);          /*set y as an (n × 1) vector distributed as
                          N(0, 1)*/
a = 1; b = 2;           /*set a and b parameters to equal 1 and 2,
                          respectively*/
y = ln(a) + (sqrt(ln(b)) * y);
                        /*yield y distributed as N[ln(a), ln(b)]*/
x = exp(y);             /*yield x distributed as L(a, b)*/
```

TABLE 2.2
Characteristics of the Lognormal,
Chi-Square, and Student's t Distributions

	Lognormal	Chi-Square	Student's t
Notation	$L(a, b)$	$\chi^2(c)$	$t(c)$
Parameters	a = median, $b > 0$	c = degrees of freedom (c an integer > 0)	c = degrees of freedom (c an integer > 0)
Probability density function	$f(x) =$ $[x\sigma(\sqrt{2\pi})]^{-1} e^{\frac{-(\log x - \mu)^2}{2\sigma^2}}$, where $\mu = \ln(a)$ and $\sigma^2 = \ln(b)$	$f(x) =$ $\dfrac{x^{(c-2)/2} e^{(-x/2)}}{2^{c/2}\Gamma(c/2)}$, where $\Gamma(k)$ is a gamma function with argument k	$f(x) =$ $\dfrac{\Gamma[(c+2)/2]}{\sqrt{\pi c} * \Gamma(c/2) * [1 + (x^2/c)]^{(c+1)/2}}$, where $\Gamma(k)$ is a gamma function with argument k
Range	$0 \leq x < \infty$	$0 \leq x < \infty$	$-\infty < x < \infty$
Mean	$a * e^{(\ln b)/2}$	c	0, if $c > 1$
Variance	$a^2 * b(b - 1)$	$2c$	$c/(c - 2)$, if $c > 2$
Skew	$(b + 2)(b - 1)^{1/2}$	$2^{3/2} c^{-1/2}$	0, if $c > 3$, but always symmetric
Kurtosis	$b^4 + 2b^3 + 3b^2 - 3$	$3 + (12/c)$	$3(c - 2)/(c - 4)$, if $c > 4$

2.2.1.3.3 The Chi-Square Distribution: $\chi^2(c)$

In Monte Carlo simulation, it often is useful to vary a variable's distributional characteristics systematically, examining the effects of this variation on the behavior of the statistic being evaluated. The use of the chi-square distribution allows a researcher to vary a variable's skew in this way. As its degrees of freedom (c) increase, the chi-square distribution changes from being extremely right-skewed to approaching symmetry and normality as its skewness goes to 0 and its kurtosis goes to 3 (Table 2.2 and Figure 2.6). Therefore, if a researcher systematically decreases the degrees of freedom from a large number (say, 20 or 30) to 1, then he or she can assess the effects of monotonically increasing skew on his or her simulation. This

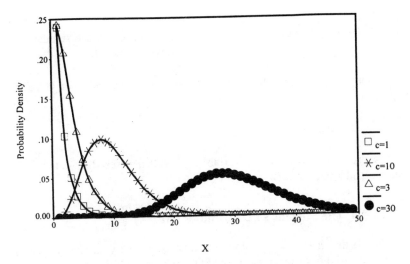

Figure 2.6. Probability Density Functions of Chi-Square (c)

can be especially useful in assessing violations of the normality assumption
(Section 4.4). A chi-square distributed variable can be converted into a
left-skewed variable by multiplying by −1.

A member of this distributional family is completely characterized by
its degrees of freedom in that the mean, variance, skewness, and kurtosis
all are functions of c. Therefore, if one varies c to change the skew, then
one also should standardize the resulting variables by subtracting the
degrees of freedom (the theoretical mean) from each case and dividing each
case by the theoretical standard deviation, $\sqrt{(2*c)}$. This will yield a variable
distributed as chi-square with a given degrees of freedom but centered on
0 with a standard deviation of 1.

A chi-square distributed variable can be constructed by summing a series
of c squared standard normal variables:

```
df = 1;                /*set the degrees of freedom, c, to 1*/
y = rndn(n,df);        /*set y as an (n × df) matrix distributed as
                         N(0, 1)*/
y = y .* y;            /*element-by-element multiplication of y to
                         square each element*/
y = y';                /*transpose y*/
y = sumc(y);           /*sum the columns of the transposed
                         matrix, yielding y distributed as χ²(c)*/
```

22

```
y = (y-df)/sqrt(2 * df);        /*set mean = 0 and standard
                                deviation = 1*/.
```

For simplicity of use in this text, I define these commands as a GAUSS procedure:

```
y = chi(df,n);
```

This procedure will yield a variable, y, with n cases distributed as a non-standardized $\chi^2(df)$.

2.2.1.3.4 The Student's t Distribution: $t(c)$

Just as the chi-square distribution can be used to vary the skewness of a random variable systematically, the Student's t distribution can be used to vary its kurtosis in the leptokurtic range while keeping symmetry. The Student's t PDF is a bell-shaped symmetrical distribution with infinitely long tails that differs from the normal distribution in that a parameter, c (the degrees of freedom), determines not only the variance but also the kurtosis of the distribution (Table 2.2). As c increases, the Student's t becomes less and less leptokurtic, approximating the standard normal distribution in the limiting case of an infinite number of degrees of freedom (Figure 2.7). The standardized Student's t is centered at 0 but can be generalized as to its mean by adding a constant to each case of the generated variable.

A variable distributed as a standardized Student's t with c degrees of freedom can be generated by dividing a standard normal variable by the square root of an independently generated chi-square variable divided by its degrees of freedom, c:

$$t(c) \sim = \frac{z}{\sqrt{y/c}} \tag{2.3}$$

where $z \sim N(0, 1)$ and $y \sim \chi^2(c)$ is independent of z. The degrees of freedom of the chi-square variable will be the degrees of freedom of the resulting Student's t distribution. In GAUSS, we proceed as follows, given $z \sim N(0, 1)$ and $y \sim \chi^2(c)$, both $(n \times 1)$ vectors:

```
x = z ./ sqrt(y/c);            /*yield x as an (n × 1) vector
                               distributed t(c)*/.
```

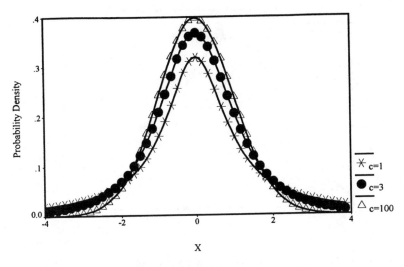

Figure 2.7. Probability Density Functions of $t(c)$

2.2.1.3.5 Mixture Distributions

Certain biological and social phenomena can be represented best by mixtures of distributions (Everitt & Hand, 1981). Phenomena that theoretically are characterized as mixtures usually are not unique characteristics but rather combinations of traits that have not been modeled completely. For example, the height of human beings is best characterized as the mixture of two normal distributions. This is because the height of women normally is distributed around a certain mean with a certain variance, and the height of men normally is distributed around another mean with another variance. Therefore, if we model height without taking gender into account, the result is a mixed normal distribution.[8]

A mixture distribution can also be used to simulate a distributional shape that cannot be generated using a standard distribution. For example, if a researcher wanted to generate a highly skewed distribution, then he or she could develop a mixture of two normal variables whose means were far apart and whose mixing proportion (the proportion drawn from each of the two variables) was very small (Figure 2.8). But, as discussed elsewhere in this chapter, there are other distributions that can be controlled more easily in their skewness (and other characteristics) than can a mixture distribution. Therefore, this use of mixture distributions may be less necessary than their fairly common use would suggest.

24

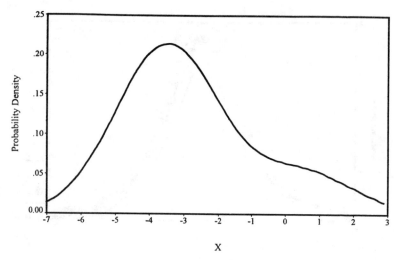

X

Figure 2.8. Probability Density Function of a Mixture of Two Normal Distributions

Any number of variables with any distributions can be mixed together, and so it is impossible generalize about the characteristics of this type of distribution. However, a key parameter common to all mixtures is the mixing proportion, p, where $0 \leq p \leq 1$. The basic generation strategy for a two-distribution mixture is to create a vector from one distribution that is n^*p in length and one from the other distribution that is $n^*(1-p)$ in length. These vectors then are vertically concatenated to yield a variable with n cases. If required, the resulting variable then can be randomized using a U(0, 1) index variable. The following GAUSS commands create a mixture of two N(a, b) variables with mixing proportion, p:

```
y1 = rndn(((1-p) * n),1);    /*set y1 as a {[(1 - p)*n] ×
                             1} vector distributed as N(0, 1)*/
mean = a1; variance = b1;    /*set mean and variance to
                             a1 and b1, respectively*/
y1 = mean + (sqrt(variance) * y1);
                             /*yield y1 distributed as
                             N(a1, b2)*/
y2 = rndn((n * p),1);        /*set y2 as a [(n*p) × 1] vector
                             distributed as N(0, 1)*/
mean = a2; variance = b2;    /*set mean and variance to
                             a2 and b2, respectively*/
```

```
y2 = mean + (sqrt(variance) * y2);
                                    /*yield y2 distributed as
                                    N(a2, b2)*/
y = y1 | y2;                        /*vertically concatenate y1
                                    and y2 into an (n × 1) vector*/
index = ceil(rndu(n,1) * n);       /*create a uniformly
                                    distributed index of
                                    integers, 1 to n*/
x = submat(y,index',0);            /*shuffle y using index,
                                    yielding x distributed as a
                                    mixture of two normals with
                                    mixing proportion, p*/
```

2.2.1.4 The Acceptance-Rejection Method

A researcher may wish to generate a variable with a distribution that neither has a tractable inverse distribution function nor is a simple function of one or more easily generated distributions. In this case, he or she may use the acceptance-rejection method of distribution generation, which is sort of an automated trial-and-error approach (Rubinstein, 1981, pp. 45-58; von Neumann, 1951). The computer draws a uniformly distributed random number, x, from the acceptable range of the desired variable along with an independent uniformly distributed random number, p, a pseudo-density value. The x then is fed into the PDF formula of the desired distribution, resulting in a density for that number given that distribution. If this calculated density is less than p, then x is accepted as coming from that distribution and placed into a vector of x's for the simulated variable. If the density is greater than p, then x is rejected. Random and independent (x, p) pairs are drawn until n x's finally are accepted.

Because some numbers will be rejected in this process for almost any distribution, the computer will draw more than n pairs of random numbers. To reduce the number of rejections and thereby increase the efficiency of the procedure, one needs to eliminate as many (x, p) pairs from the potential selection region as possible. This is done by "boxing off" the (x, p) region that could potentially be chosen from a given PDF, thereby shrinking the "rejection region." To do this, first limit x to the potential range for the desired distribution, thereby defining the "width" of the box. Therefore, x will be selected from a U(min, max) distribution, where min and max are the minimum and maximum of the potential range of the desired distribution. For many distributions, of course, either or both of these values is (are) infinite, in which case a practical limit needs to be defined. For example, an L(1, 3) distributed variable could range from 0 to infinity, but one could limit the upper end to, say, 10 so as to proceed with the acceptance-rejection procedure, given that the chances of observing a value greater than 10 from such a distribution are tiny.[9] This means that the acceptance-rejection method is more efficient for truncated distributions with fat tails than it is for ones with long thin tails.

The second step in setting up the box of potential (x, p) pairs is to define the box's "height" as the maximum value of the density in the PDF. Every PDF has a modal value(s) of x, which can be determined analytically or from a standard reference book (e.g., Evans et al., 1993; Johnson & Kotz, 1970a, 1970b). The modal value for x is fed into the PDF, yielding the maximum density. For example, if we feed 0 (the mode) into the PDF formula for an N(0, 1) distribution (Table 2.1), we get .399, the maximum density in the normal distribution. For each potential x, this maximum density is multiplied by a scalar drawn randomly from a U(0, 1) distribution. This yields p, which is distributed as U(0, maximum density). Graphically, this cuts out the entire rejection region that is the open-topped rectangle tangent to and above the PDF at the maximum density.

The efficiency of the acceptance-rejection method therefore is affected by the shape of the PDF. The greater the ratio of the highest to lowest points on the PDF, the more cases are rejected and the less efficient the acceptance-rejection method. This is because the maximum value of the PDF determines the top of the box area from which the (x, p) pairs are drawn. If there are places on the PDF that are considerably lower than the maximum, say at the tails or at the middle of a bimodal distribution, then there will be more much rejection space in the boxed-off region. A uniform variable, on the other hand, has no point on the PDF higher than any other point, and so no x's are rejected.

Even given these considerations, however, the acceptance-rejection method sometimes is even faster than a composition method that requires the creation of multiple variables for a single resultant variable such as a chi-square distribution with many degrees of freedom. Furthermore, there are more efficient ways in which to develop an acceptance-rejection algorithm such as enveloping the desired distribution within two closely related distributions (Schmeiser & Shalaby, 1980), which is a more thorough way to box off the potential (x, p) space. The straightforward approach that I demonstrate for the beta distribution is easy to program and provides an efficient way in which to generate bounded distributions.

TABLE 2.3

Characteristics of the Beta Distribution

Notation	Bet(a, b)
Parameters	$a\ (a > 0),\ b\ (b > 0)$
Probability density function	$f(x) = \dfrac{x^{a-1}(1-x)^{b-1}}{\beta(a,b)},$
	where $\beta(a,\ b)$ is the beta function with arguments a and b
Range	$0 \le x \le 1$
Mode	if $a > 1$ and $b > 1$, then $(a-1)/(a+b-2)$, otherwise 1 and/or 0
Mean	$a/(a+b)$
Variance	$\dfrac{ab}{(a+b)^2(a+b+1)}$
Skew	$\dfrac{2(b-a)\sqrt{a+b+1}}{(a+b+2)\sqrt{ab}}$
Kurtosis	$\dfrac{3(a+b)(a+b+1)(a+1)(2b-a)}{ab(a+b+2)(a+b+3)} + \dfrac{a(a-b)}{a+b}$

2.2.1.4.1 The Beta Distribution: Bet(a, b)

The beta is a very flexible distribution that is bounded by 0 and 1 (although these bounds can be changed as in Section 2.2.1.1). It has two parameters, a and b, and its moments and functions are defined in Table 2.3. The beta is useful for social science simulations because it is extremely flexible, with its PDFs ranging from highly right-skewed, to uniform, to approaching normality, to highly left-skewed, and even to bimodal distributions with varying levels of interior "dip" (Figure 2.9). The shape is determined by the values of the parameters. For example, a Bet(1, 2) PDF is a straight line with a negative slope, whereas a Bet(2, 1) is a straight line with a positive slope. A Bet(1, 1) is a uniform distribution, and any beta where $a = b$ and the parameters are large approximates normality. When either a or b is below 1, the PDF curves downward from one end of the

28

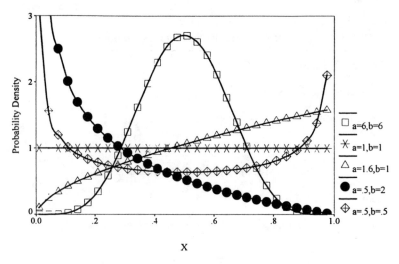

Figure 2.9.   Probability Density Functions of Bet(a, b)

range; when both a and b are below 1, the PDF is bimodal. The ratio of the height of these modes to the central portion in a bimodal distribution is increased by decreasing a and b toward 0. The beta is symmetric if a and b are the same value and will be asymmetrical to the extent that the parameters diverge. Therefore, within the range of its potential values, the beta distribution can be used to simulate a host of social science variables and can be used to vary the shapes of PDFs systematically in a variety of ways.

Generating a Bet(a, b) variable is a straightforward application of the general acceptance-rejection procedure. First, one determines the maximum density by calculating the modal value of x using a, b, and the PDF formula (Table 2.3).[10] Next, the x value to be "tried out" for a case of the variable and a random probability, u, are drawn independently. Because the range of beta is from 0 to 1, x is drawn from a U(0, 1) distribution, as is u. The density at the mode then is multiplied by u to yield p,[11] and x is transformed into a density by running it through the PDF. The resulting density is compared to p, and x is included in the generated variable vector if this density is less than p; otherwise, it is rejected. This procedure continues until n x's are included in the generated variable. The following GAUSS code returns a Bet(6, 6) variable with 10,000 cases:

29

```
/*Set parameters*/
n = 10000;
a = 6; b = 6;                /*set beta parameters*/
i = 1;                       /*set index for cases*/
x = zeros(n,1);              /*set an empty vector to hold
                             accepted trial values of x*/
```
/*Calculate beta(*a*, *b*) function using the gamma function, and set the
    peak value of *p**/
```
beta = (gamma(a) * gamma(b))/gamma(a + b);
if a > 1 and b > 1;          /*start calculations to find the mode
                             of the distribution*/
  mode = (a-1)/(a + b-2);    /*calculate the mode of Bet(a, b)*/
 peak = (mode^(a-1)) * ((1-mode)
    ^(b-1))/beta;            /*calculate PDF value at mode*/
 else;
   peak = 4;                 /*see Note 11*/
endif;
do until i > n;              /*start do loop to go through cases*/
```
/*Draw two U(0, 1) numbers*/
```
 p = rndu(1,1) * peak;       /*density to use in accept/reject
                             procedure*/
 trial = rndu(1,1);          /*number between 0 and 1 to use as
                             the potential x value*/
```
/*Calculate f(trial) and compare to *p*, accepting or rejecting*/
```
 function = (trial^(a-1)) *
   ((1-trial)^(b-1))/beta;
 if prob <= function;        /*compare random probability
                             scalar to potential x*/
   x(i,1) = trial;           /*accept trial as an x value if
                             condition is met*/
   i = i + 1;                /*increment i if trial is accepted*/
 endif;
endo;
```

For simplicity of use in this text, I define these commands as a GAUSS procedure:

TABLE 2.4

Monte Carlo Experiments on the Efficiency of Acceptance-Rejection
Generation of Bet(*a, b*) Variables (percentages)

Distribution	Cases Rejected
Bet(10, 10) (approaching normality)	53.7
Bet(5, 5)	41.2
Bet(2.5, 2.5)	24.9
Bet(1.5, 1.5)	11.6
Bet(1, 1) (uniform)	0.0
Bet(.75, .75)	75.0
Bet(.5, .5)	76.1
Bet(.1, .1)	89.1
Bet(.05, .05) (highly peaked, bimodal)	93.3

NOTES: $N = 10,000$ for all experiments. All distributions are symmetric, given that $a = b$. Peak density
for $a < 1$ experiments was set at 4.0.

```
y = bet(a,b,n);
```

This command would yield a variable, y, with n cases distributed as Bet(a, b).

As already noted, the efficiency of acceptance-rejection is related to the ratio of the highest to the lowest points in the PDF being generated. This can be seen in Table 2.4, where several examples of the percentage of rejected cases are displayed. These are the results of simulations to generate 10,000 cases of each of the given beta distributions, and they show that upward of 50% of cases can be rejected when large portions of the potential (x, p) space are in the rejection region. The level of rejection is especially high for distributions in which a and/or b are (is) less than 1 because the peak density is infinite and a fairly high practical level of the density needs to be set in a simulation (see Note 11). But note that for simple simulations, efficiency really is not much of a practical concern. For example, to simulate 10,000 cases from a Bet(.05, .05), even with a 93.3% rejection rate, an IBM clone with a Pentium 133 processor took only 30 seconds.

2.2.2 Discrete Distribution Functions

Whereas a continuous random variable can take on any value in its range, a discrete random variable can only take on certain specific values. These discrete values generally are positive integers, although this can be adjusted in a variable by multiplying and/or adding a constant. These distributions are especially useful for simulating counts of states, that is, the number of times a particular state has existed for a unit of analysis: the number of marriages a person has entered into, the number of times a person has entered the hospital, a person's gender (the state of being male or female), the number of "aye" votes in a committee, the number of wars in which a country has engaged, and so on.

Most of the discrete distributions discussed in this monograph are generated as some combination of Bernoulli trials. Bernoulli trials are independent and identical "experiments" with a dichotomous outcome in which the probability of a "success" or "failure" in each experiment is the same. The classic example of a Bernoulli trial is a single coin toss, with a success being if it comes up heads. These trials then are combined in different ways to yield a variety of distributions. The distribution function with which a variable should be generated is determined by the ways in which these trials are combined in the social process being simulated.

Most of the probability theory and notation discussed for continuous distributions is the same for discrete distributions. The main difference is that the distribution function now is the *sum* of $p(X \leq x)$, rather than the integral of the probabilities, because X now can take on only certain values within the range. Following this, the analog of a continuous distribution function's PDF is called the *probability mass function* (PMF) for a discrete distribution function.

2.2.2.1 The Bernoulli Distribution: Ber(p)

If a variable is generated by a process with only two outcomes and with a constant probability of these outcomes occurring across cases, then that variable has a Bernoulli distribution. Gender is the classic example. But properly conceptualized into complementary categories, many social conditions can be thought of as being Bernoulli distributed: voted Labor/not Labor, college degree/no college degree, passed a test/did not pass. This distribution can be used to generate the many dummy variables used in the social sciences with the assumption of constant probability across cases.

The Bernoulli distribution has a range of two values, 0 and 1, and it has one parameter, p, the probability of any case equaling 1 (Figure 2.10). Its mean is p and its variance is $p(1-p)$ (Table 2.5). The skewness and kurtosis also are determined by the parameter p.

To simulate a Ber(p) variable, x, generate an ($n \times 1$) vector, y, from a U(0, 1) distribution to simulate probabilities. Then compare these simulated probabilities to the parameter, p, giving x a value of 1 if $y \leq p$ or 0

TABLE 2.5
Characteristics of the Bernoulli and Binomial Distributions

	Bernoulli	Binomial
Notation	Ber(p)	B(t, p)
Parameters	$p = \text{pr}(x = 1)$, $(0 \leq p \leq 1)$	t = number of trials (an integer > 0), $p = \text{pr}(x = 1)$, $(0 \leq p \leq 1)$
Distribution function	$F(0) = 1 - p$, $F(1) = 1$	$F(x) = \sum_{i=0}^{t} \binom{t}{i} p^i (1-p)^{t-i}$
Probability mass function	$f(0) = 1 - p$, $f(1) = p$	$f(x) = \binom{t}{x} p^x (1-p)^{t-x}$
Range	0,1	$0 \leq x \leq t$, where x is an integer
Mean	p	tp
Variance	$p(1-p)$	$tp(1-p)$
Skew	$\dfrac{1-2p}{\sqrt{p(1-p)}}$	$\dfrac{1-2p}{\sqrt{tp(1-p)}}$
Kurtosis	$\dfrac{1}{p(1-p)} - 3$	$3 - \dfrac{6}{t} + \dfrac{1}{tp(1-p)}$

otherwise. In GAUSS, a vector of values equal to p needs to be generated to make the comparison casewise with y:

```
prob = .4;              /*set p(x = 1) to .4*/
y = rndu(n,1);          /*set y as an (n × 1) vector
                          distributed as U(0, 1)*/
pv = prob * ones(n,1);  /*set pv as an (n × 1) vector of
                          the scalar, p*/
x = (y .<= pv);         /*set x to 1 if y ≤ pv, yielding x
                          distributed as Ber(.4)*/
```

For simplicity of use in this text, I define these commands as a GAUSS procedure:

```
y = ber(p,n);
```

This command would yield a variable, y, with n cases distributed as Ber(p).

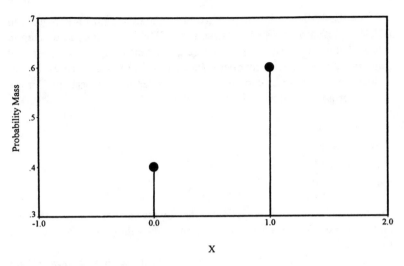

Figure 2.10.   Probability Mass Function of Ber(.6)

2.2.2.2 Multichotomous Variables

Many social science variables have more than two natural categories
(e.g., race, religion, party voted for) or are constructed this way from
continuous variables (e.g., categories of income, educational attainment,
national economic development). These variables are similar to dummy
variables in that they are categorizations, but they are not Bernoulli
distributed because there are more than two possible outcomes. Although
there is no standard distribution family from which these variables are
drawn, they can be simulated if the probability of a case falling into each
category, the PMF, can be specified. For example, to simulate a "race"
variable for a study of the U.S. population, a researcher might determine
from empirical studies that

$p(x = \text{white} = 1) = .75$
$p(x = \text{black} = 2) = .12$
$p(x = \text{Hispanic} = 3) = .08$
$p(x = \text{other} = 4) = .05.$

Note that the sum of the probabilities of all the outcomes for this PMF is
1.0, as must be true of any PMF or PDF.

Once the PMF has been specified, a cumulative distribution function (CDF) is developed. When constructing a CDF, it is important to keep in mind whether the variable is ordinal (e.g., income categories) or nominal (e.g., race). The category number values are arbitrary in both cases, but for ordinal variables the categories should be ordered appropriately. For the "race" variable in the preceding, the CDF is

$$p(x \le 1) = .75$$
$$p(x \le 2) = .87$$
$$p(x \le 3) = .95$$
$$p(x \le 4) = 1.0.$$

The range of such a variable is determined by the category values assigned, and the mean and variance can be determined by the general formulas for these parameters.

A variable with a CDF specified in this way then can be generated with the inverse transformation method. This is done by drawing a pseudo-probability scalar, y, from a U(0, 1) for each case and constructing a series of IF statements in the computer algorithm to classify a case according to the point in the CDF at which y falls. In GAUSS,

```
let mult_dis = .75 .87 .95 1.0;   /*set a vector of the desired
                                     CDF as in the "race" variable*/
x = zeros(n,1);                   /*set x as an empty (n × 1) vector*/
i = 1;                            /*set case index */
y = rndu(n,1);                    /*set an (n × 1) vector of values
                                     from U(0, 1)*/
 do until i > n;                  /*begin loop to go through cases*/
  if y[i] <= mult_dis[1];         /*test if y (for case i) is in the first
                                     category*/
   x[i] = 1;                      /*if so, then set the variable to
                                     equal 1*/
  elseif y[i] <= mult_dis[2]);
                                  /*continue testing for each
                                     category*/
   x[i] = 2;
    elseif y[i] <= mult_dis[3];
    x[i] = 3;
    else;
```

```
    x[i] = 4;        /*if y is not in categories 1-3, then it must be
                       in 4*/
  endif;             /*end loop for case i*/
  i = i + 1;         /*increase case index*/
endo;               /*yield a four-category multichotomous
                       variable with the CDF specified in mult_dis*/
```

2.2.2.3 Distributions Arising From Combinations of Bernoulli Trials

The binomial, Poisson, and negative binomial distributions all can be thought of as combinations of series of Bernoulli trials. As such, they can be generated with a very similar generic approach using the inverse transformation method[12]:

1. Set $i = 0$.
2. Set $i = i + 1$, and for Case x_i conduct the following steps:
3. Generate a number, u, from a U(0, 1).
4. If $u \leq p(x = 0)$, then set $x_i = 0$ and return to Step 2.
5. If $u > p(x = 0)$, then calculate $p(x = 1)$ and add this to $p(x = 0)$. This creates the cumulative probability, $p(x \leq 1)$.
6. If $u \leq p(x \leq 1)$, then set $x_i = 1$ and return to Step 2.
7. If $u > p(x \leq 1)$, then continue calculating $p(x = k)$ and adding it to the previous probabilities to create $p(x \leq k)$ until $u \leq p(x \leq k)$.
8. Set $x_i = k$ and return to Step 2.
9. Stop when $i > n$.

The basic idea is very similar to that for generating multichotomous variables. For each integer value from 0 upward, there is a probability that a variable with a given distribution function will take it on. For each case, a random number, u, from U(0, 1) simulates a randomly generated probability. To determine which value of the discrete variable is associated with this probability in a specified distribution function, we first calculate $p(x = 0)$ for that distribution. If that probability is greater than u, then we calculate $p(x = 1)$ and add it to $p(x = 0)$. In other words, we construct a CDF and find the category (the value of x) associated with the probability chosen at random. This is done on a case-by-case basis because cases with different values of u will proceed through the system to different levels of the $k + 1$ categories.

TABLE 2.6
Characteristic Components for Generating
Discrete Distributions Using the Generic Algorithm

	Notation	GAUSS Code
Binomial: B(t, p)		
p_init	$(1-p)^t$	(1-p)^t
p_factor	$\dfrac{(t-k)p}{(k+1)(1-p)}$	(((t-k)*p)/((k+1)*(1-p)))
Poisson: P(λ)		
p_init	$e^{-\lambda}$	exp(-lambda)
p_factor	$\dfrac{\lambda}{k+1}$	(lambda/(k+1))
Negative binomial: NB(f, p)		
p_init	p^f	p^f
p_factor	$\dfrac{(f+k)(1-p)}{k+1}$	(((f+k)*(1-p))/(k+1))

SOURCE: Rubinstein (1981, p. 99).

The key to constructing such an algorithm is to be able to calculate $p(x \leq k)$, as defined by the distribution function. Therefore, the generic computer code for generating a binomial, Poisson, or negative binomial variable is the same, with substitutions for $p(x = 0)$, p_init, and the factor to increase the probability at each step, p_factor, being the only changes (Table 2.6):

```
case = 1;           /*set the case index counter*/
do until case > n; /*start the case-by-case looping*/
p0 = p_init;        /*set the distribution-specific starting value of
                      p*/
c = p0; b = p0;     /*set necessary internal parameters to the
                      initial p value*/
k = 0;              /*set k (category number) to 0 to start*/
y = rndu(1,1);      /*set y as a U(0, 1) scalar*/
if y <= b;          /*begin loop to set xi value*/
x[case,1] = k;      /*set xi = 0 if y ≤ p(x = 0)*/
```

```
else;
  do until y <= b;      /*start loop to increase p(x ≤ k)
                          incrementally*/
  c = c*p_factor;       /*using the distribution-specific p_factor,
                          calculate p(x = k + 1)*/
  k = k + 1;            /*increase k to the next level*/
  b = b + c;            /*add p(x = k + 1) to p(x ≤ k), creating the
                          cumulative distribution function for the
                          new k*/

    if y <= b;
      x[case,1] = k;    /*set x_i = k if y exceeds the new
                          cumulative distribution function*/

    endif;
  endo;                 /*otherwise, return to do to increment b
                          again*/

  endif;
    case = case + 1;    /*increment case number*/
endo;                   /*return to do until n cases are generated,
                          yielding x as an (n × 1) vector with the
                          specified distribution*/.
```

Other discrete distributions that can be simulated in this way include the geometric, hypergeometric, and logarithmic series distributions.

2.2.2.3.1 The Binomial Distribution: $B(t, p)$

A variable is binomially distributed if it is the sum of the successes of a series of t Bernoulli trials. That is, if a given event with a dichotomous outcome is repeated t times and the probability of a success remains constant at p, then the number of successful events is distributed binomially. The parameters of this distribution are t, the number of trials in the "experiment," and p, the probability that any trial will yield a success. This distribution is an extension of the Bernoulli into t trials, which is indicated in that the difference between the means and variances of these distributions is a factor of t (Table 2.5). The PMF varies with parameters t and p (Figure 2.11), and its range is the integers from 0 to t. Its generation follows the generic inverse transformation approach discussed previously.

The binomial distribution may be appropriate for simulating a variable that is the sum of t random dichotomous events. For example, it might be used to simulate how many of the past four semesters a student could not

38

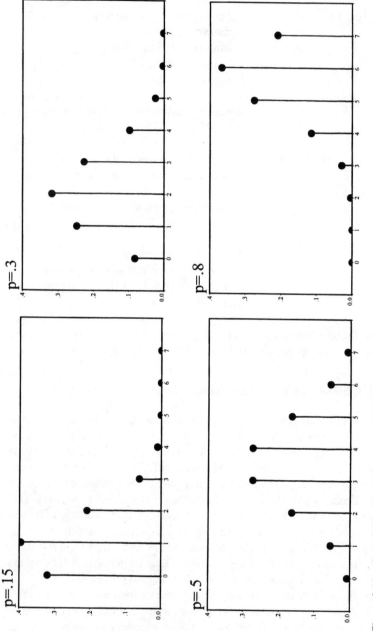

Figure 2.11. Probability Mass Functions of B($7, p$)

enroll in a class due to overcrowding. The assumption that p is constant across all trials can be a factor limiting the use of the binomial in the social sciences, however. For example, the probability that a congressperson votes "aye" on a term limits measure probably is affected by his or her previous votes on the issue. King (1989, pp. 45-48) suggests relaxing the assumption of constant p and instead assuming that p is beta distributed, resulting in an extended beta-binomial distribution for the final variable. A straightforward composition generating approach could yield such a variable. First, one would generate a beta distributed value of p for each trial and then construct a binomial distribution using this probability. The binomial distribution has much wider and more plausible application in gaming (where its study originated), genetics, engineering, and animal ecology (Johnson et al., 1992, pp. 134-135).

As t gets large, the iterative generation procedure can become time consuming for the binomial distribution because the number of potential x values whose probability must be assessed is equal to $t + 1$. Fortunately, for large t, the normal distribution provides a good approximation of the binomial. Rubinstein (1981, p. 102) suggests using the normal approximation when $tp > 10$ (for $p > .5$) or when $t(1 - p) > 10$ (for $p \leq .5$). To generate a binomially distributed variable from $y \sim N(0, 1)$ in such a case, solve the following formula for each case in x:

$$x = \text{Max}\{0, [-.5 + tp + y\sqrt{tp(1 - p)}]\}, \qquad (2.4)$$

where $[m]$ denotes the integer part of m.

2.2.2.3.2 The Poisson Distribution: $P(\lambda)$

The Poisson distribution characterizes counts of dichotomous event outcomes occurring in a given period, such as the number of presidential vetoes in a year. Again, the key assumption underlying this distribution is that the probability of an event occurring is constant across time and trials. The parameter specifying the member of the Poisson family to which a given process belongs is λ, which is the rate of success. That is, if $\lambda = 4$, then we can expect that there will be four events in the time period defined by the process, be it an hour, a day, or a year. Therefore, the mean of the Poisson distribution is λ, as is its variance (Table 2.7). Because a Poisson distributed variable is a count, its range consists of the positive integers from 0 to infinity.

Counts per time arise quite often in social science data: the number of car accidents on a highway in a month, the number of trips to the doctor in

TABLE 2.7
Characteristics of the Poisson and Negative Binomial Distributions

	Poisson	*Negative Binomial*
Notation	$P(\lambda)$	$NB(f, p)$
Parameters	λ = rate of success ($\lambda > 0$)	$f > 0$ and an integer, p = probability of Bernoulli success ($0 \leq p \leq 1$)
Distribution function	$F(x) = \sum\limits_{i=0}^{x} \lambda^i e^{-\lambda}/i!$,	$F(x) = \sum\limits_{i=1}^{x} \binom{f+i-1}{f-1} p^f (1-p)^i$
Probability mass function	$f(x) = \dfrac{\lambda^x e^{-\lambda}}{x!}$	$f(x) = \binom{f+x-1}{f-1} p^f (1-p)^x$
Range	$0 \leq x < \infty$, x is an integer	$0 \leq x < \infty$, x is an integer
Mean	λ	$f(1-p)*p^{-1}$
Variance	λ	$f(1-p)*p^{-2}$
Skew	$\lambda^{-1/2}$	$(2-p)[f(1-p)]^{-1/2}$
Kurtosis	$3 + \lambda^{-1}$	$3 + \dfrac{6}{f} + \dfrac{p^2}{f(1-p)}$

a year, the number of customers at a store in a day, the number of specified words in a book chapter, and so on (Haight, 1967, Chapter 7). Often these are treated as continuous variables, but this can lead to nonsensical results with, for example, predictions of negative and noninteger numbers. For example, how would one interpret a prediction that -1.3 cars were sold by a salesperson in a week?

The generation of a Poisson distributed variable can proceed generically with the inverse transformation method already described. When λ is large, however, another approach can be taken. The skew of a Poisson distributed variable decreases as λ increases (Figure 2.12), and once $\lambda > 10$ the normal distribution provides a good approximation. At this point, a Poisson distributed variable can be generated with a normal approximation in a fashion similar to that for the binomial:

$$x = \text{Max}(0, [-.5 + \lambda + \sqrt{y}]), \qquad (2.5)$$

where $y \sim N(0, 1)$ (Rubinstein, 1981, p. 103).

41

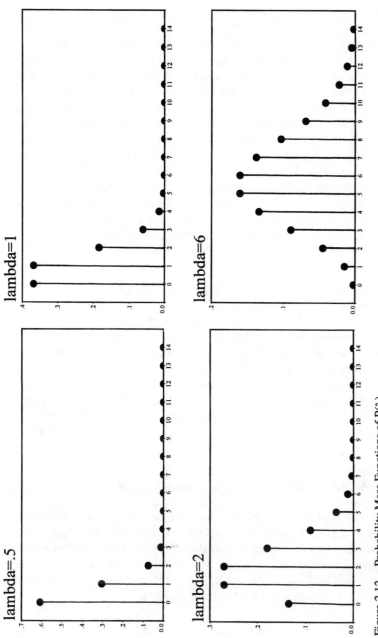

Figure 2.12. Probability Mass Functions of $P(\lambda)$

2.2.2.3.3 The Negative Binomial Distribution: NB(*f*, *p*)

The assumption of the Poisson process of a constant p is unrealistic in count data for many social science variables. For example, the rate of incumbent defeat in state legislative elections likely varies from year to year, as might the rate of out-of-town trips per year for families. In fact, arguments could be made for a nonconstant p for all the examples discussed in the previous section. The negative binomial distribution allows for the generation of a variable drawn from a mixture of Poisson distributions in this way (Greenwood & Yule, 1920). This is done by assuming that λ is a random variable with a gamma$\{f, [p/(1 - p)]\}$ distribution, resulting in a negative binomial distribution with two parameters, a positive number, f, and the probability of success in a trial, p (Rubinstein, 1981, p. 106).[13] This distribution then acts like a mixture of Poisson distributions whose λ's vary as a gamma. Therefore, the range is the same as in the Poisson and the moments are quite similar except for the insertion of f (Table 2.7 and Figure 2.13).

2.3 Generating Combinations of Random Variables

Up to this point, I have discussed only the generation of individual, independent variables. But when developing a simulation of a social process, it usually is necessary to generate multiple variables that are related to one another in some fashion. The relationships among the variables should follow directly from substantive theory regarding the process and/or theory regarding the statistical procedures being evaluated. Two general types of variable relationships are discussed here: model-based relationships and variables that follow multivariate distributions. The distinction between these two is practical and pedagogical rather than theoretical.

2.3.1 Model-Based Relationships Among Variables

Almost invariably, the social process being simulated involves a relationship between two or more variables. In the extreme case, two variables are perfectly correlated with one another if one variable is a perfect function of the other. The difference between x and y will be that of a scale factor if x is multiplied by a constant to arrive at y, and the scale of x will be shifted from that of y if a constant is added to x to yield y:

$$\text{scale factor, } \beta: y = \beta * x$$
$$\text{shifting constant, } \alpha: y = \alpha + x. \tag{2.6}$$

43

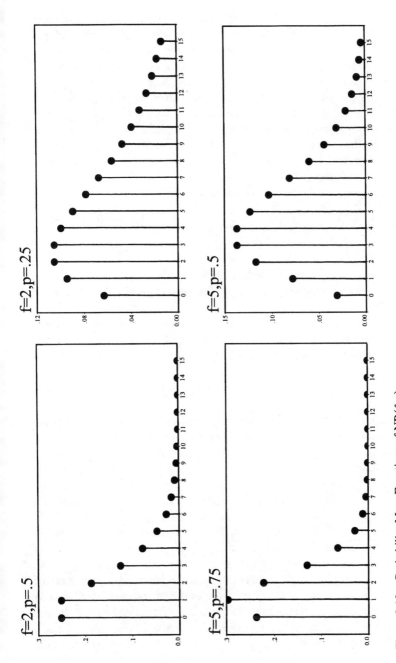

Figure 2.13. Probability Mass Functions of NB(f, p)

Here x and y are perfectly correlated, but they will differ in variance (with a scale factor) or mean (with a shifting constant). If the scale factor is negative, then the correlation between x and y will be negative. To simulate this, one simply generates x in any fashion desired and then creates y by adding or multiplying a constant. Because the only variable aspect of the creation of this y is in x, y will be in the same distributional family as x.

Models using perfectly correlated variables usually are of little interest in the social sciences because most social relationships are stochastic. However, these deterministic relationships can easily be turned into stochastic relationships with the inclusion of a random variable in the model. This random component, or "error term," can be added to x or multiplied by x to create y, as dictated by substantive theory:

$$y = x + \varepsilon \text{ or}$$
$$y = x * \varepsilon, \tag{2.7}$$

where ε = a random variable independent of x.

This random component breaks up the perfect relationship between x and y. The level to which the correlation is reduced depends on the size of the error relative to the scale of x. In generating such a model, the researcher should add a multiplicative weight, w, a scalar whose value can be manipulated to adjust the level of correlation between x and y:

$$y = x + (\varepsilon * w). \tag{2.8}$$

Another important consideration in generating a stochastic model of the relationship between x and y is the distribution function of ε. This should be determined by substantive theory when possible, or perhaps a variety of distributions varying in some interesting fashion may be employed in successive models. For example, a researcher might vary the skew of ε across a series of experiments by employing the chi-square distribution with a range of degrees of freedom. As already noted, however, even within the same family different distribution functions can have different expected values and variances, and therefore varying ε's distribution may result in different levels of correlation between x and y, even with a constant w. Because the expected value of the chi-square distribution is its degrees of freedom, in this example the relative size of the error term will increase as the degrees of freedom increase. The variance of the chi-square distribution also changes with the degrees of freedom. As noted in Section 2.2.1.3.3, the way in which to solve this problem, and thereby retain control of the relative size of ε, is to standardize each case of ε by subtracting the *theoretical mean* value of the distribution and dividing by the *theoretical standard deviation* before multiplying it by w. This will ensure that $E(\varepsilon) = 0$ and $SD(\varepsilon) = 1$, regardless of its distribution.

At this point, it should be clear just how closely these models are tied to regression models, the most commonly used statistical models in social science. In fact, a bivariate regression model is simply the expression of all of the aspects of relationships discussed in this section: multiplying a variable, x, by a constant and adding a constant and a random variable to generate another variable, y. This can easily be extended to multiple regression by adding more x's being multiplied by constants. An indicator of the overall correlation between y and the x's in the model is R^2. This can be controlled most easily in a model by adjusting the relative size of the error term with the weight, w. This is most easily done on a trial-and-error basis to arrive at the R^2 desired to simulate a given process. The level of correlation among the x's also can affect the R^2 value.

The extension of a multiple regression model to a multiequation model is straightforward. If a variable, g, is the dependent variable in one model and an independent variable in another model, then one generates the model with g as the dependent variable first and then uses the resulting g in the second model as an independent variable. The control of the R^2's of the models becomes increasingly complex with the increase in the complexity of the equation systems, but otherwise there is no theoretical problem with extending the system indefinitely, at least for recursive models. The simulation of nonrecursive systems is more problematic, however, in that there will be at least two variables whose values are needed to generate each other. One approach to take here is to simulate a two-stage (or more) least squares model, simulating instrumental variables for one of the reciprocally related variables in each pair.

The following GAUSS code combines all of the aspects of model-based relationship generation discussed in this section into the simulation of a two-equation, multiple-regression model with chi-square distributed error. The model to be simulated is

$$y_1 = \alpha_1 + \beta_1 x_1 + \beta_2 x_2 + \varepsilon_1 \qquad (2.9)$$
$$y_2 = \alpha_2 + \beta_3 x_3 + \beta_4 y_1 + \varepsilon_2,$$

where $\operatorname{cov}(\varepsilon_1, \varepsilon_2) = 0$. In the following code, $e1$ and $e2$ have been generated previously as chi-square distributed variables with degrees of freedom $df1$ and $df2$, respectively:

```
cases = n;                          /*set sample size to n*/
beta1 = b1; beta2 = b2;
beta3 = b3; beta4 = b4;             /*set slope parameters as
                                       constants*/
alpha1 = a1; alpha2 = a2;           /*set intercept terms as
                                       constants*/
w1 = weight1; w2 = weight2          /*set error weights*/
x1 = seqa(0,1,n);                   /*x1 generated additively
                                       from 0 and increasing by
                                       ones*/
x2 = rndn(n,1);                     /*x2 is set as an (n × 1) vector
                                       from N(0, 1)*/
x3 = rndu(n,1);                     /*x3 is set as an (n × 1) vector
                                       from U(0, 1)*/
y1 = alpha1 + (beta1 * x1) + (beta2 * x2) +
(((e1-df1)/sqrt(2 * df1)) * w1);
                                    /*set y1 as a function of x1
                                       and x2 with standardized
                                       and weighted chi-square
                                       error*/
y2 = alpha2 + (beta3 * x3) + (beta4 * y1) +
(((e2-df2)/sqrt(2 * df2)) * w2);
                                    /*set y2 as a function of x3
                                       and y1 with standardized and
                                       weighted chi-square error*/.
```

This code yields $y1$, $y2$, $x1$, $x2$, and $x3$ having the specified stochastic relationships.

2.3.2 Multivariate Relationships Among Variables

Just as a single variable, x, has a distribution function that plots the cumulative probability associated with every potential value of x, a set of variables, say x and y, has a multivariate distribution function that plots the cumulative probability of observing sets of values, (x, y). Such a distribution is based on (a) the distributions of the individual variables and (b) the relationship between the variables. Any set of variables has a multivariate distribution, but when the variables are independent of one another, this distribution contains no more information about them than their individual distribution functions. Furthermore, even if the variables are related, their multivariate distribution function may not take on a standard form. There has been far less theoretical work done on multivariate distributions than there has on univariate distributions; therefore, the choices as to standard, well-understood functions are limited (Johnson, 1987, pp. 2-4). Regardless of this, the development of sets of variables with specified multivariate distributions can be very useful in simulation work, particularly in setting correlation matrices with much greater precision than can be done with the model-based approach.

2.3.2.1 The Multivariate Normal Distribution

A pair of variables are multivariate normally distributed if each of the variables is normally distributed. The distribution function for a set of p variables is denoted $N_p(\mu, \Sigma)$, with the parameters μ, a $(p \times 1)$ vector of means, and Σ, the $(p \times p)$ covariance matrix of the variables. The three-dimensional representation of the PDF of a pair of such variables has a "cowboy hat" appearance, with the shape becoming more eliptoid as the variables become more correlated (Johnson, 1987, pp. 51-54). The principal usefulness of this distribution for the social scientist is that it allows him or her to specify the correlations among the variables in a simulation.

To simulate a multivariate normal distribution among p variables with n cases, a researcher first generates an $(n \times p)$ matrix of values from the N(0, 1) distribution, **Y**. To set the correlation matrix for the variables in the columns of **Y**, **cor**, a $(p \times p)$ matrix, **A**, is constructed such that $\mathbf{AA'} = \mathbf{cor}$. This can be done by setting up a matrix of correlation values as desired for **cor** and then taking its Choleski decomposition, which is akin to taking the square root of the matrix (Johnson, 1987, pp. 52-54). This can be done algebraically, which becomes very tedious as the number of variables increases past two, or with the convenient chol command in GAUSS. Once **A** has been constructed, **X**, an $(n \times p)$ matrix whose columns are distributed as $N_p(0, \mathbf{cor})$, is developed:

$$\mathbf{X} = \mathbf{Y} * \mathbf{A}. \qquad (2.10)$$

The correlation matrix, **cor**, is equivalent to the covariance matrix, Σ, at this point because the variables are standardized to means of 0 and variances of 1. Note also that all the correlations must be positive at this point. To generate negatively correlated variables, follow this procedure up to this point and then multiply one of the variables to be negatively correlated by –1 while still standardized.

To set the means of the columns of **X** as desired, add an $(n \times p)$ matrix of means to **X**, where each column contains only the desired mean of the variable in the corresponding column of **X**. A similar procedure is run to set the variances of the columns of **X**, except that one multiplies cellwise the matrix of standard deviations by **X** rather than adding them to **X**. Note that these scaling and shifting transformations do not affect the correlations among the x's.

To construct a matrix of multivariate normally distributed variables in GAUSS:

```
k = 3;                         /*set number of variables. (Note: If
                               changed from 3, then adjust other
                               parameters and the A matrix
                               development accordingly)*/
let means = 23 34 2.1;    /*set means*/
let sds = 3.4 56.1 .03;   /*set standard deviations*/
r12 = .25; rd13 =.75; r23 = .5;
                               /*set correlations  among variables*/
means = (means * ones(1,n))';
                               /*set means matrix to be (n × k)*/
sds = (sds * ones(1,n))';      /*set standard deviation
                               matrix to be (n × k)*/

/*Set up A matrix*/
a = ones(k,k); a[1,2] = r12; a[1,3] = r13;
    a[2,1] = r12; a[2,3] = r23; a[3,1] = r13;
    a[3,2] = r23;
a = chol(a);                   /*take the Choleski factorization
                               of A*/

/*Set multivariate normal distribution: Nk(mu, sigma^2)*/
x = rndn(n,k);
x = x * a;
x[.,1] = x[.,1] * -1;     /*set r12 and r13 to be negative*/
x = means + (x .* sds); /*yield Nk(means, sds^2)*/
```

The generated variables now are the columns of the **X** matrix, having the specified correlations, means, and standard deviations.

2.3.2.2 Other Multivariate Distributions

It may be necessary to construct sets of variables with a specified correlation matrix but that are not all normally distributed. This may be useful, for example, in testing the effects of multicollinearity on OLS regression slope estimates or in simulating a set of test scores to be factor analyzed. To construct such a set of variables, the general procedure just described for setting the correlation matrix for a multivariate normal distribution is followed. That is, one sets the pseudo-population correlation matrix, calculates **A**, and then multiplies this by the **X** matrix of standardized variables. The means and standard deviations can be set as desired after the correlation matrix has been set. The following GAUSS commands will generate a set of three variables, two with normal distributions and one with a uniform distribution, with the desired correlation matrix specified by **A** (see the multivariate normal commands for specifying **A**):

```
y1 = rndu(n,1);      /*set y1 distributed as U(0, 1)*/
y1 = (y1-.5)/sqrt(1/12);
                     /*standardize y1 by its theoretical mean and
                     standard deviation*/
y2 = rndn(n,1); y3 = rndn(n,1);
                     /*set y2 and y3 as independent
                     variables distributed N(0, 1)*/
y = y1~y2~y3;        /*horizontally concatenate yi's to create y
                     matrix*/
y = y * a;           /*set the correlation matrix of y using a
                     matrix previously defined*/
x = (y .* sds) + means;
                     /*set means and standard deviations of the
                     columns in the x matrix to be as previously
                     defined*/
```

A problem with this procedure is that it tends to "normalize" the variables that are in the right-hand columns of **X**. That is, because of the algebra of the procedure, a standardized $\chi^2(1)$ variable looks more like a $\chi^2(5)$ variable after the preceding procedure if it is in the far right column of **X**. This effect is more pronounced the farther to the right in **X** a variable is placed. Therefore, any highly nonnormal variables should be placed in the left-hand columns of **X**. Because this problem is exacerbated the farther to the right in **X** a variable is located, it is difficult to generate a large number of correlated nonnormal variables with this procedure.

50

3. USING THE PSEUDO-POPULATION
IN MONTE CARLO SIMULATION

In Chapter 2, I described how to generate the various components of a pseudo-population. In this chapter, I discuss how to put these pieces together into a pseudo-population that can be used in a simulation to assess the characteristics of statistical estimators.

3.1 An Example of a Complete Pseudo-Population Algorithm

A pseudo-population algorithm must be developed to reflect the reality of a data gathering and analysis situation as accurately as possible in all relevant respects. This requires careful consideration of both the social processes being simulated and the sampling and statistical techniques used by the researcher. In this section, I demonstrate how to simulate a very simple social process, showing how the components described in Chapter 2 fit together.

The situation to be simulated is this. Dolores Delfeld, a political scientist, is interested in explaining state legislators' attitudes toward government regulation of business. She developed a 0-100 scale to measure this variable and surveyed a random sample of 50 legislators on the issue. The researcher hypothesized that party affiliation, income, and educational attainment would have independent effects on this attitude, and so she wanted to fit a multivariate regression model to the data using OLS. However, there was some question as to the normality of the distribution of the dependent variable (and therefore the error term), and with this small sample the accuracy of parametric inference was in question. She therefore wished to simulate the process with the goal of assessing the accuracy of parametric inference for this situation (Section 4.4).

The first step in any simulation is to write out the complete statistical model and define its components as fully as possible, using the researcher's theoretical and empirical knowledge of the relationships and variables involved. In this case, the model is

$$y_i = \alpha + \beta_1 x_{1i} + \beta_i x_{2i} + \beta_3 x_{3i} + \varepsilon_i. \tag{3.1}$$

Examining real data estimates of similar models and assessing similar variables' characteristics are good ways in which to get ballpark values for the pseudo-population characteristics. In this example, the researcher, after examining her data and considering previous research on the subject, determined that x_1 (party) should be a dummy variable with a population percentage of 53% equaling 1, x_2 (income) should be a lognormally distributed variable with a mean of 35,000 and a standard deviation of 27,000, and x_3 (educational attainment) should be a standard normal variable. The correlation between x_1 and the other x_k's needed to be .00, and the correlation between x_2 and x_3 needed to be .70. The error term, ε, should be highly skewed to the right to reflect the skew of y in her data. To reflect her sample data, the R^2 of the model should be about .40, the sample size should be 50, and a simple random sample should be used. Finally, she determined that the following values for the model parameters were reasonable: $\alpha = 1$, $\beta_1 = 15$, $\beta_2 = .0001$, and $\beta_3 = 2$.

The next step in developing a pseudo-population algorithm is to translate this description into computer code. First, the constants are set to the values required. Then, the error term is generated, say with a chi-square distribution with 2 degrees of freedom, standardized to have a mean of 0 and a standard deviation of 1. A weighting factor, w, is included to adjust the R^2. Trial and error will need to be undertaken to determine the exact value needed for w. The matrix of independent variables consists of four columns, one for each variable in the model and one column of ones for the constant term. The vector of dummy variables for x_1 is constructed from a Ber(.53) distribution. The other two independent variables first are constructed independently with a mean of 0 and a standard deviation of 1 but with a lognormal and normal distribution, respectively. These are standardized to set the correlation between them to .70 using the A matrix procedure, after which the mean and standard deviation of x_2 can be set to 35,000 and 27,000, respectively.

In GAUSS, the following will generate such a pseudo-population:

```
/*Set parameter values*/
n = 50;                          /*set sample size*/
let beta = 1 15 .0001 2;         /*set population slope
                                   coefficients*/
w = 10;                          /*set error weight value*/
p = .53;                         /*set proportion for x₁ = 1*/
df = 2;                          /*set degrees of freedom for
                                   chi-square error term*/
r23 = .7;                        /*set correlation between x₂ and
                                   x₃*/
mn_x2 = 35000; sd_x2 = 27000;    /*set parameters for x2*/

/*Set up the chi-square distributed error term, e*/
e = chi(df,n);                   /*yield e distributed χ²(df)*/
```

52

```
e = (e - df)/sqrt(df * 2);/*set E(e) = 0 and sd(e) = 1*/
e = e * w;                  /*weight e with w*/

/*Set up the x matrix*/
x0 = ones(n,1);             /*set vector of ones for intercept
                              term*/
x1=Ber(p,n);                /*yield x1 distributed as Ber(p)*/
x2 = rndn(n,1);             /*begin lognormal generation for x2*/
x2 = exp(x2);
x2 = (x2 - exp(.5))/sqrt(exp(1)* (exp(1) - 1));
                            /*standardize x2*/
x3 = rndn(n,1);             /*set x3 distributed as N(0, 1)*/

/*Set correlation between x2 and x3 using A matrix procedure*/
a = ones(2,2);
a[2,1] = r23; a[1,2] = r23;
a = chol(a);
x_cor = x2 ~ x3;
x_cor = x_cor * a;
x_cor[.,1] = (x_cor[.,1]
* sd_x2 + mn_x2;           /*set scale and mean of x2*/

/*Final y variable development*/
x = x0~x1~x_cor;           /*build an (n × 4) x matrix*/
y = (x * beta) + e;        /*set an (n × 1) vector of y values*/.
```

3.2 Generating a Vector of Monte Carlo Estimates

If one were to run the preceding commands in GAUSS, the output that would be useful for a simulation experiment would be the last three columns in the **x** matrix (the independent variables) and the $(n \times 1)$ vector of y. These data would be a single realization, a *pseudo-sample*, of the pseudo-population as defined by the computer algorithm. However, if we estimate the regression coefficients of the model by running OLS on these data (as in Table 3.1), we will get numbers that undoubtedly are not equal to the parameter values set in the computer algorithm. Comparing the estimates to the parameters in Table 3.1 indicates obvious discrepancies, some of them very large indeed. This does not mean that I have programmed the computer incorrectly (although this possibility needs to be checked); rather, it is a reflection of the fact that the process being modeled

TABLE 3.1

Ordinary Least Squares Regression of Y on $\mathbf{X}$ for a Single Run
of the Example Pseudo-Population Generating Algorithm

Parameter	Pseudo-Population Value[a]	Pseudo-Sample Value[b]
α	1.0	–4.638
		(2.52)
β_1	15.0	16.834
		(2.31)
β_2	.0001	.0002
		(.00006)
β_3	2.0	–1.972
		(1.44)
ρ_{23}	.70	.80
μ_{x1}	.53	.44
μ_{x2}	35,000	41,616.41
μ_{x3}	.0	.246
σ_{x1}	.499	.501
σ_{x2}	27,000	34,254.36
σ_{x3}	1.0	1.345

NOTE: $N = 50$; $R^2 = .37$. Standard errors of the ordinary least squares estimates are in parentheses.
a. Value set for the parameters in the pseudo-population generating computer algorithm (Section 3.1).
b. Estimate calculated from a single pseudo-sample drawn using the pseudo-population algorithm.

is stochastic rather than deterministic. When a sample of data is drawn from
a real population and a statistical model is estimated, the resulting estimates
are stochastically different from the underlying true parameter values, and
this process is simulated in Monte Carlo within the computer. (Table 3.1 is
a good example of why simulators quickly gain a healthy respect for
random variation and a strong skepticism about the "truth" imbued in point
estimates by some researchers.)

The singular advantage of Monte Carlo simulation over real data in this
respect is that with Monte Carlo simulation we can draw *hundreds* or even
thousands of samples with the same ease with which we can draw one
sample. What is of interest in Monte Carlo studies is the behavior of a
statistic over many, many pseudo-samples or *trials*. As stated in Section
1.1, the basic strategy is to draw a pseudo-sample, conduct the estimation
technique, save the estimate of interest ($\hat{\theta}$), draw another pseudo-sample,
conduct the estimation technique, save $\hat{\theta}$, and so forth for t trials. The result
is a ($t \times 1$) vector of $\hat{\theta}$'s whose relative frequency distribution is the Monte
Carlo estimate of the sampling distribution of that statistic in that particular
statistical situation. This sampling distribution then can be evaluated in a

54

variety of ways to help understand the behavior of $\hat{\theta}$, as discussed in Chapter 4.

But first, how does one generate all these thousands of pseudo-samples and estimate the sampling distribution of some statistic, $\hat{\theta}$? Once the computer algorithm to generate a single pseudo-sample has been written, the generation of multiple trials is a simple matter. The technique is to take the entire algorithm, from data generation to statistical estimation, and place it into a *looping procedure*. This will instruct the computer to continue executing the sampling and estimation procedures until the required number of trials has been completed.

To do this, the required number of trials is defined first. Then, an index scalar, t, is set to 1. In some programs, such as GAUSS, an empty vector needs to be defined at the outset to be filled with $\hat{\theta}$ from each trial. Finally, a do until (or similar) command is used to tell the computer to continue undertaking the procedures between this and the endo command until t equals the number of trials required. Near the end of the do loop, directly after the estimation procedure, $\hat{\theta}$ is placed into the vector of Monte Carlo estimates. In GAUSS, this is done by indexing the estimate into the vector with the trial number as the row number in the estimate vector. Then, the trial index, t, is increased by 1 (otherwise the loop never would end, as it is waiting for t to equal the preset number of trials required). Finally, an endo (or similar) statement is required to end the loop once the condition regarding the value of t set at the beginning of the loop has been met. All this usually requires less than 10 lines of code bracketing the generating algorithm.

Consider the pseudo-population discussed in Section 3.1. If the statistic of interest there is the OLS estimate of β_2, then here is how GAUSS would generate a $(t \times 1)$ vector of β_2's. First, the following commands would be placed *before* the pseudo-population generating algorithm but *after* the pseudo-population parameters are set:

```
t = 1;                       /*start the index t at 1*/
mc_trials = 500;             /*order 500 Monte Carlo trials*/
beta2 = zeros(mc_trials,1)   /*set beta2 as an empty
                             vector to hold estimates*/
do until t > mc_trials;      /*start the do loop, to end
                             when t > mc_trials*/
```

At this point, the pseudo-population generating code (Section 3.1) is inserted. To get the OLS estimate of interest, the pseudo-sample y is regressed on the pseudo-sample **x** (stripped of the first column, which contains the ones needed for the constant term in the generation of **y**). The resulting β_2 is placed in the tth row of the Monte Carlo vector for this statistic. The index, t, then is incremented by 1, and the end of the loop command is given. It also is good practice to insert a `print` command after a loop has been completed to monitor the process, especially if the looped procedures are complex and time consuming and if many trials are to be run:

```
/*Regress y on the x matrix, saving the OLS estimates as the vector,
    beta*/
{vnam,m,beta,stb,vc,stderr,sigma,cx,rsq,resid,dw}
    = ols(0,y,x);
let beta2[t,1] = beta[3,1];
                        /*set the tth row of the beta2 vector as the
                        current OLS estimate*/
print "Trial" t;        /*outputs this message after each trial*/
t = t + 1;              /*increment t by 1*/
endo;                   /*end the do loop*/.
```

3.3 Generating Multiple Experiments

Just as multiple trials can be generated using a looping procedure, so too can multiple experiments. For example, a researcher may wish to assess the distribution of OLS $\hat{\beta}$s from similar models with a range of ρ_{23}'s to evaluate the effect of multicollinearity (Section 4.4). This could be done by embedding the entire Monte Carlo experiment algorithm into *another* looping structure. This would be similar to that used for trial replication in that a `do until` structure would be used with an index indicating the experiment number as the condition. The difference would be that, along with incrementing the experiment index after each experiment, one also would increment the relevant parameter value by a specified amount. In this example, a researcher might start with $\rho_{23} = .95$ and decrease it by .05 with each experiment until $\rho_{23} = .05$.

This procedure can take a considerable length of time to execute, especially if the model and its estimation procedures are complex. If one experiment requires t repetitions of the sampling and estimation procedure, then a loop for e experiments requires $(t*e)$ repetitions. This sort of procedure therefore may best be done on a mainframe computer or on a dedicated personal computer (or when one is going on vacation!). But more important, one must be certain that the program is written as desired because it cannot be checked until the entire process is completed. It is especially important to check that the parameter(s) one varies across the experiments have the desired effects. It often is the case in simulation studies (as in real social processes) that a change in one condition has repercussions for other conditions in the system, and sometimes these conditions are not apparent without careful examination of the output of the process. For instance, by varying the correlation between x_2 and x_3 in the example, the R^2's will vary if this is not controlled for with some change in w as the experiments progress. The general point is that one should undertake looped experiments only with a well-understood model of a social process and a well-understood computer algorithm. However, in situations where such well-developed theory and algorithms exist, looping experiments can be a very efficient way to proceed.

3.4 Which Statistic Is to Be Saved From a Trial?

At this point, consider the issue of which statistic to save from each trial of an experiment. Of course, this is entirely dependent on the question being studied, and although this is taken up in greater detail in Chapter 4, it is useful here to consider several possibilities. First, as in the previous example, a researcher may wish to save the point estimate of a population parameter. This could be used to assess the estimator's bias, efficiency, distributional shape, or certain percentiles, as discussed in Section 3.6.

Another quantity that can be saved from a trial is a *counter* variable, which assesses the presence or absence of a particular state in a given pseudo-sample. For example, a researcher may wish to note whether or not an estimate is higher than a certain value. This can be useful in assessing an inferential technique, say, to see how often a test statistic exceeds a critical value. Two sets of procedures are required to develop a counter variable. First, an empty vector is defined prior to the loop to hold the value from each trial:

```
counter=zeros(mc_trials,1);
```

Then, within the loop, after the data generation and estimation procedures, an if-then procedure is used to score the tth row of the counter variable as 1 if the condition is true for the trial and 0 if it is not. For example, in using the code in Section 3.1, if a researcher wanted to know whether the proportion of trials that r_{23} in the pseudo-samples was less than .5, then the following code could be inserted anywhere between the **A** matrix procedure and incrementing t:

```
cx = corrx(x_cor);    /*set cx as the correlation matrix for x2
                        and x3*/
if cx[2,1] < .5;      /*set the condition that causes the
                        execution of the next command*/
counter[t,1] = 1;
else;                 /*if the above condition does not hold, then
                        execute the following command*/
counter[t,1] = 0;
endif;                /*end the loop*/.
```

This will result in a $(t \times 1)$ vector of zeros and ones, depending on whether or not r_{23} was less than .5 in each trial.

Often it also is necessary to save quantities from the trials for diagnostic rather than substantive interest. For example, in Section 3.1, the researcher wanted to have the simulation achieve an average R^2 of .40. But because the error term and the independent variables were generated randomly, the value of the R^2 will vary from trial to trial even with the same pseudo-population. Furthermore, its expected value cannot be set in a straightforward manner (as can the slope coefficients) because R^2 results from a combination of several conditions. Therefore, finding the error weight that provides the desired R^2 is a matter of trial and error. Upon setting the parameters of the model as desired, a researcher will try an error weight, w, and save the R^2's for the trials. If the average of these is as desired, then that weight is used; if not, then the weight is adjusted and the procedure is repeated.

3.5 How Many Trials Are Needed?

Once the generation and estimation procedures have been programmed, the next question is, How many trials are needed in a single Monte Carlo experiment? In the early history of simulation (the 1940s through the 1960s), this was an important question because (a) the engineering and atomic physics processes being simulated often were highly complex and (b) computers of the era were very slow indeed (Hammersley & Handscomb, 1964, Chapter 1). This led to two situations. First, Monte Carlo experiments tended to be run with a very limited number of trials, and few experiments were undertaken. Second, much theoretical work was undertaken on techniques to make Monte Carlo experiments more efficient, with the development of several so-called "variance reduction techniques." These techniques can increase the efficiency of simulations; however, given the incredible speed of computers available on the desks of most social scientists today, their use in any but the most complex simulations now probably is far less important than it was previously. On the other hand, efficient simulation methods still may be important even with modern computers as more and more complex problems are tackled. (See Rubinstein, 1981, pp. 121-153, and Ross, 1990, Chapter 8, for reviews and descriptions of these variance reduction techniques.)

There are no general theoretical guidelines for the number of trials required for experimental results to be valid; conditional on the proper programming of the simulation, Monte Carlo results are unbiased for any number of trials (Hope, 1968). On the other hand, the *power* of any statistical test or comparison increases with sample size because the efficiency of a test statistic increases with sample size. If we consider each trial to be a case in a data set, then the more trials we generate, the smaller the standard deviation of any test statistic because sample size is inversely related to this standard deviation. This means that Monte Carlo experiments have greater power with more trials. But this increase in power is diminishing, as the relationship between the standard deviation of a test statistic and sample size generally is on the order of $1/\sqrt{n}$.

Another important consideration in determining the number of trials for an experiment is the nature of the results desired. For instance, the more work that is being done on the "thin" parts of a distribution (e.g., the tails), the more trials are needed. This is because values of variables and/or statistics will occur in these areas much less frequently than they will in the "thicker" sections of a distribution. Many more trials are needed to flesh out these sections fully. This means that an evaluation of the Type I error rate of a nominal .05 α-level hypothesis test would require many more trials than would an evaluation of a statistic's bias because the former deals with the tails of a distribution and the latter works on the central part (in unimodal and reasonably symmetric distributions).

The best practical advice on how many trials are needed for a given experiment is "lots!" Most simulations published recently report upward from 1,000 trials, and simulations of 10,000 to 25,000 trials are common. Many trials are used because massive computer power now is available, and many are needed because we most frequently work with the very thin tails of distributions in social science simulations. My advice is to develop programs and do exploratory analysis with as few trials and cases as possible (e.g., 1-100) but to undertake the full-blown experiments with as many trials as possible (e.g., 1,000-25,000). This will reduce wasted time early on in the process but increase statistical power in the crucial testing phases.

3.6 Evaluating Monte Carlo Estimates of Sampling Distributions

Once the simulation algorithm is written, checked, and run, the result usually is a vector of $\hat{\theta}$'s, $\hat{\theta}$, the relative frequency distribution of which is the Monte Carlo estimate of the sampling distribution of $\hat{\theta}$ in the specified statistical situation. How then can we *use* this estimate to understand the behavior of $\hat{\theta}$?

3.6.1 Evaluating the Output of a Single Experiment

Because the relative frequency distribution of the simulated $\hat{\theta}$'s is an estimate of the sampling distribution of $\hat{\theta}$, the basic characteristics of that distribution can be quite informative. The *central tendency* of the distribution lets us estimate a statistic's *bias*:

$$\text{Bias} = E(\hat{\theta}) - \theta. \qquad (3.2)$$

Because θ is known (as set in the computer algorithm), $\hat{\theta}$'s bias can be estimated by taking the mean of the $\hat{\theta}$'s and subtracting θ from it. The *variability* of a statistic can be assessed by simply taking the standard deviation of the vector. This then may be used to compare two statistics in terms of *efficiency*, for example. The *mean-squared error* of a statistic could be generated by creating a vector of θ, subtracting this casewise from the vector of $\hat{\theta}$'s, squaring this difference, and then averaging the resulting vector. If b was the statistic saved from t trials in a $(t \times 1)$ vector, then the following GAUSS code would generate each of these evaluative statistics:

```
mean_b = meanc(b)      /*yield the mean of the b vector*/
sd_b = stdc(b);        /*yield the standard deviation of the b
      vector*/
theta_v = theta * ones(t,1);
                       /*set up a (t × 1) vector of theta values, the
                       population parameter of which b is the
                       estimate*/
sq_dif = (b - theta_v)^2;
                       /*yield a vector of squared differences of b
                       from theta*/
msd = meanc(sq_dif);/*yield the mean-squared deviation
                       of b*/
```

Certain percentile values of $\hat{\theta}$ also may be of interest, especially when examining inferential tests. For example, a researcher may wish to know the value of the 2.5th percentile point to see how this compares to the parametric $\alpha = .05$ confidence interval endpoint. Any percentile value (*per*) can be obtained by (a) sorting $\hat{\theta}$'s in ascending order and (b) selecting the ([*per*/100]*t) case from that vector. If ([*per*/100]*t) is noninteger or 0, then it needs to be rounded to the nearest positive integer. Many trials are required if a percentile value in a tail of the distribution is needed. Furthermore, the more trials, the less likely that rounding error in the index will be consequential. GAUSS code to extract the *per*th percentile point from a ($t \times 1$) vector of estimates, **b**, would be as follows:

```
sort_b = sortc(b,1);          /*sort b based on Column 1
                               (the only column here)*/
per_t = ceil((per/100) * t);  /*set the case number
                               associated with per for
                               this t*/
per_b = sort_b[per_t,1];      /*select the per_t case from
                               the sorted vector of b*/.
```

The functional form of the estimated sampling distribution of $\hat{\theta}$ also may be of interest, for example, when the assumption of normality about this distribution has to be made for parametric inference. A first pass at understanding this function is to set up a simple histogram of $\hat{\theta}$ and assess it for obvious skewness and/or kurtosis deviations from normality. Again, more trials will give a clearer picture of this distribution. Skewness and kurtosis coefficients can give a more precise estimate:

$$\text{Skew Estimator } \sqrt{\hat{\beta}}_1 = \frac{\sum_{i=1}^{t} (\hat{\theta}_i - \hat{\theta}_{(.)})^3 / t}{\left(\sum_{i=1}^{t} (\hat{\theta}_i - \hat{\theta}_{(.)})^2 / t \right)^{3/2}} \tag{3.3}$$

$$\text{Kurtosis Estimator } \hat{\beta}_2 = \frac{\sum_{i=1}^{t} (\hat{\theta}_i - \hat{\theta}_{(.)})^4 / t}{\left(\sum_{i=1}^{t} (\hat{\theta}_i - \hat{\theta}_{(.)})^2 / t \right)^2}$$

$$\text{where } \hat{\theta}_{(.)} = \frac{\sum_{i=1}^{t} \hat{\theta}_i}{t}, \tag{3.4}$$

where t is the number of trials. For a normally distributed $\hat{\theta}$, the expected value of the skew is 0 and the kurtosis is 3, but sample estimates will fluctuate around these. The Jarque-Bera omnibus test combines the skew and kurtosis estimators to allow probability-based inferences about the normality of $\hat{\theta}$ (Jarque & Bera, 1987):

$$W = n * \left[\frac{\hat{\beta}_1}{6} + \frac{(\hat{\beta}_2 - 3)^2}{24} \right] \sim \chi^2_{df=2}. \tag{3.5}$$

The null hypothesis is that $\hat{\theta}$ is distributed normally. The problem with using this and other goodness-of-fit tests is one of low power. Furthermore, as a chi-square test, the Jarque-Bera is affected by sample size, so that the large experiments that are the norm in Monte Carlo simulation may show a deviation from normality more often than is justified.

For t trials and a vector of estimates, **b**, the following GAUSS code calculates the skewness and kurtosis coefficients, the Jarque-Bera test statistic, w, and gives the probability value of obtaining the observed value of w if **b** is normally distributed:

```
m1 = b - meanc(b);       /*center b*/
m3 = sumc(m1^3)/t;       /*set m3 as the third moment of b*/
m4 = sumc(m1^4)/t;       /*set m4 as the fourth moment of b*/
var_b = sumc(m1^2)/t;    /*set the variance of b*/
skew = m3/(var_b^1.5);   /*calculate skewness
                           coefficient*/
kurt = m4/(var_b^2);     /*calculate kurtosis coeficient*/
```

```
w = t * (((skew^2)/6) + (((kurt - 3)^2)/24));
```
    /*calculate w, the Jarque-Bera test statistic for normality*/
```
prob_w = cdfchic(w,2);
```
    /*yield the probability value for w from a χ^2 ($df = 2$)
    distribution*/.

For simplicity of use in this text, I define these commands as a GAUSS
procedure:

```
{skew,kurt,w,prob_w} = jarqbera(test_variable,n);
```

For a variable with n cases, test_variable, this command will return the
estimated skewness and kurtosis coefficients, Jarque-Bera test statistic, and
probability that the data were drawn from a normally distributed population
variable.

3.6.2 Evaluating the Output of Multiple Experiments

One problem with interpreting the results of Monte Carlo simulations is
specificity; that is, the results of a single experiment apply only to the
statistical situation explicitly specified by the pseudo-population (Hendry,
1984).[14] Would the statistic behave differently if the sample size, correlation matrix of the independent variables, error distribution, or something
else were different? With the massive increases in computer power of the
past decade or two (Mooney & Krause, in press), Monte Carlo experiment-
ers now can address this problem by executing a variety of experiments
under a variety of conditions. The mechanics of this sort of procedure were
discussed in Section 3.3. In this section, I discuss some considerations in
designing and analyzing multiple experiments.

Because it only recently has become feasible to run multiple Monte Carlo
experiments of any complexity, there has been little discussion about
experimental design principles in the context of these studies (Johnson,
1987, p. 6; but see Kleijnen, 1975, Chapter 4). But there appear to be at
least two central issues that a researcher must consider carefully in designing these experiments: the multiplicity of potential sources of variation and
the interdependency of these sources.

The factors that may influence experimental outcomes often are numerous and can include sample size, each variable's distribution function,
correlation among the variables, and the level and distribution of the
stochastic component. Furthermore, each of these components has a wide

range of potential variation. For example, a single variable could be generated by numerous functions, and each of these functions could have a variety of parameter values. And the number of potential *combinations* of factor characteristics increases multiplicatively. For example, in a bivariate regression simulation, using only three distributions for x and three for the error term yields nine unique combinations to be simulated. Because of this situation, the following admonition needs restatement: A researcher needs to understand the social process he or she is attempting to simulate to the fullest extent possible. This is essential here to hold constant those factors of which he or she is relatively certain and to vary only those factors that are in some way contentious theoretically. Any variability that is outside the realm of plausibility or that does not affect the experimental output of interest needs to be eliminated. For instance, in the bivariate regression example, if it is clear that the independent variable is uniformly distributed in the real world, then the researcher ought not vary its distribution in the simulations.

The other problem that arises when designing a set of Monte Carlo experiments is that often the factors hypothesized to influence the experimental results are interdependent. For example, changing the level of heteroskedasticity in a regression model will affect its average R^2 because of changing squared error levels. In experimental design, the goal is to vary factors *independently* to identify independent effects, and so the experimenter needs to control this interdependence across experiments. As noted in Section 2.2.1.3.3, using different distribution functions for variables often will change the expected value and variance. This problem is addressed by using standardized variables, which then can be reconverted to their original metrics as required. Other times, an ad hoc procedure may need to be developed to reduce the interdependence across experiments. In the heteroskedasticity/R^2 example, if the problem is that R^2 falls as heteroskedasticity increases, then the researcher could include a decrement to the error weight in the experiment loop to reduce the error as heteroskedasticity increases.

Having addressed these concerns, the next step in designing a multiple experiment simulation is to specify an output variable(s) for each experiment. This usually will be a scalar (or set of scalars) that evaluates the estimated sampling distribution of $\hat{\theta}$ according to the research question. Section 3.6.1 describes a few obvious candidates: the estimate of $\hat{\theta}$'s bias, mean-squared error, skewness, kurtosis, and the probability of it being normally distributed. Other evaluative statistics discussed in Chapter 4 are the observed levels of Type I and Type II inferential error and the differences between competing estimates. The point is to define statistical output for each experiment that estimates the property that the researcher finds interesting. This estimate then is collected and stored for each experiment.

The values of the characteristics of the experiment that are hypothesized to influence the evaluative statistic also should be collected and stored for each experiment. For example, if it is hypothesized that increasing levels of correlation among the independent variables of a regression model will increase the mean-squared error of the OLS slope estimates, then the value of this correlation for each experiment needs to be collected and stored. Experimental factors to be saved can either be estimated from the pseudo-sample data (e.g., average R^2) or set by the pseudo-population (e.g., sample size).

This experimental output now can be organized into a data matrix, such that each row is the output from one experiment and the columns are the factors saved from each experiment. It is quite natural, then, to analyze these data as one would analyze data from a physical experiment in which one variable is thought to be a function of a variety of other variables—regression analysis, where the dependent variable is the evaluative statistic and the independent variables are the experimental factors. However, as is often the case in experimental research, there may not be good theoretical reason to specify a functional form for the relationship between the dependent and independent variables in Monte Carlo experiments. One could just run a linear OLS model, but what if the effect of, for instance, R^2 on mean-squared error is curvilinear?

One approach to overcoming this problem of functional indeterminacy that has been used widely with other types of experimental data is *response surface analysis* (RSA) (Hendry, 1984). RSA is a procedure that employs OLS regression to explore the relationship between y and $\mathbf{x}$ using progressively more complex polynomial models until a satisfactory fit to the data is found (Box & Draper, 1987). This involves beginning with a linear model, moving to a second-level polynomial with squared x terms and all possible bivariate interactions among the x's, then moving to the third-level polynomial, and so on:

$$\begin{aligned} \text{First Order: } y &= \alpha + \beta_1 x_1 + \beta_2 x_2 + \varepsilon \\ \text{Second Order: } y &= \alpha + \beta_1 x_1 + \beta_2 x_2 + \beta_{11} x_1^2 + \beta_{22} x_2^2 \\ &\quad + \beta_{12} x_1 x_2 + \varepsilon. \end{aligned} \quad (3.6)$$

Fit will improve monotonically by definition as higher level polynomials are used, but it is easy to see that even with just a few experimental factors, the degrees of freedom for the model will be depleted rapidly. This is less of a problem for Monte Carlo experimentation than it is for physical experimentation, however, because usually it requires far fewer resources to replicate the former than the latter.

At what point do we stop increasing the complexity of the model and accept a given specification? Box and Draper (1987, pp. 275-278) suggest a criterion that uses the observed F statistic of the model. They suggest that one can accept a given specification as adequate when $F_{ob} > (F_{\alpha}*10)$. At this point, one can be assured that the relationships embodied in the data have been adequately teased out by the analysis. The fit of the RSA model, summarized in the R^2, will be dependent on the amount of random variation embedded in the pseudo-population generating processes that led to the experimental data.

All the usual specification tests should be conducted to assess the plausibility of OLS assumptions on the final RSA model. Heteroskedasticity often is a problem (Hendry, 1984), but this can be rectified by estimating White (1980) standard errors for the slopes in making inferential tests.

The output of an RSA can be interpreted like the output of any regression analysis. A statistically significant slope indicates that that factor or interaction has a nonzero effect on the evaluative statistic in the direction indicated by the sign of the coefficient. However, because the interactions and polynomial terms of even a second-order model can make the interpretation of the overall effect of an experimental factor difficult, it often is useful to graph the predicted value of the performance statistic across values of a factor. Such a plot often will show the curvilinear aspects of the relationship between the independent and dependent variables more clearly than will simply the estimated coefficients. See Sections 4.4 and 4.5 for examples of RSA and the graphical and tabular display of its output.

4. USING MONTE CARLO SIMULATION IN THE SOCIAL SCIENCES

In Chapters 2 and 3, I described the components of Monte Carlo simulation and showed how to execute simulation experiments. In this chapter, I bring together these mechanics and describe a variety of situations in which Monte Carlo simulation can be used in the social sciences. The uses of simulation outlined in this chapter are neither mutually exclusive nor exhaustive; rather, they are offered for pedagogical and suggestive purposes only. There undoubtedly are many more uses to which simulation can be put by creative social scientists, as the potential of this technique is only just beginning to be explored. Two such uses not discussed in this chapter are in Bayesian and bootstrap statistical inference (Efron & Tibshirani, 1993; Gelman, Carlin, Stern, & Rubin, 1995) and in teaching statistics (Mooney, 1995; Simon & Bruce, 1991).

4.1 Inference When Weak Statistical Theory Exists for an Estimator

Standard parametric inference requires a high level of statistical theory about an estimator. An analytic proof as to its sampling distribution under conditions such as are encountered in the data is needed, as are formulas to estimate the parameters of this distribution from sample data. When it works, this approach to inference is precise and easy to use, and that is why it is the dominant inferential paradigm in the social sciences today. But there are situations in which this approach cannot be applied. First, the conditions under which a proof is developed may not hold in a given situation. For example, the well-known OLS regression assumptions must hold for those slope estimators to be minimum variance and linear unbiased, according to the Gauss-Markov theorem. When these conditions do not hold, we cannot be certain of the properties of these estimators. In Section 4.4, I describe how Monte Carlo simulation can be used to assess the effect of the violation of these assumptions on parametric inference.

The second situation in which the analytical mathematics of parametric inference fail is when a statistic has no well-developed statistical theory regarding its distribution under any conditions. This is the situation I consider in this section. Sometimes a researcher may wish to use a statistic that seems to meet his or her substantive needs for a problem but about whose distribution little is known. In such a case, it is difficult to have confidence in either the point estimate or any inference to a population value based on this statistic. For example, Bartels (1993, p. 274) uses a ratio of correlated regression coefficients to make important statements about the impact of the media on people's perceptions of presidential candidates. This "new," custom-made statistic speaks clearly to his substantive concerns; unfortunately, there exists no statistical theory for him to use in assessing his point estimates. Is his estimator unbiased? What is its sampling distribution? Analytical statistical theory offers little guidance here.

This situation is becoming more common as social scientists gain more statistical expertise and move away from their reliance on the few statistics and models for which strong statistical theory exists. Indeed, aside from the sample mean and those statistics derived from it, such as OLS regression coefficients, there are few statistics with strong, general statistical theory associated with them (Efron & Tibshirani, 1993, p. 12). Examples of estimators with weak statistical theory that already are used in the social sciences include indirect paths in causal models, eigenvalues, the switch point in switching regression models, and the difference between two medians. Furthermore, many combinations of statistics, such as Bartels' estimator or Jackman's "vote bias" estimator (discussed later), fall into this category.

Monte Carlo simulation can be used to understand the behavior of these sorts of statistics in the following way. If we know (or are willing to make assumptions about) the components that make up a statistic, then we can simulate these components, calculate the statistic, and explore the behavior of the resulting estimates. In this way, the pseudo-population is the set of component variables of the statistic. It may well be the case that we have more information about the behavior of the variables that go into a model than the parameter estimators themselves. For example, Jackman (1994, p. 327) creates an estimator of the percentage of the votes needed by a minority party in a two-party system to gain 50% of the legislative seats, "vote bias"[15]:

$$\text{Estimate(Vote Bias)} = \frac{\exp(-est.\{\log[\beta]\}/\hat{\rho})}{1 + \exp(-est.\{\log[\beta]\}/\hat{\rho})}, \qquad (4.1)$$

where

$$\log(y_i) = \log(\beta) + \rho * \log(x_i) + \ln(\varepsilon_i). \qquad (4.2)$$

Equation 4.2 models the relationship of the minority-to-majority party seats ratio (y) as a function of the minority-to-majority party votes ratio (x), using a natural log transformation (Schrodt, 1982). Although Jackman's vote bias estimator provides a straightforward and important interpretation of the bias in a two-party system (Kendall & Stuart, 1950), its statistical properties cannot be understood theoretically, especially in the small samples generally used in empirical research in this area. But because we know something about the distribution of the variables that are used in the calculation of the estimator, we can use Monte Carlo simulation to explore the vote bias estimator's properties experimentally.

The first step in conducting such an experiment is to understand the data and model to be simulated. If we were trying to examine the vote bias estimator's properties for the U.S. House elections of 1932-1988, for example, then the components of the pseudo-population should be as shown in Table 4.1. We would generate these components, combine them accord-

TABLE 4.1
Characteristics of the Pseudo-Population
for the Vote Bias Estimator Evaluation Experiment

Variable	Mean	Standard Deviation	Distribution
Minority votes	45.66	3.26	Normal
Majority votes	52.81	3.04	Normal
ε	0	1.0	Normal

NOTE: Constant values: $\log(\hat{\beta}) = -.152$, $\hat{\rho} = 1.942$, sample size = 29, $R^2 = .744$. The parameters in this table were set for Equation 4.2 based on fitting U.S. House elections data (1932-1988) to the votes/seats model.

ing to Equation 4.2, and calculate the vote bias estimate as in Equation 4.1. Multiple trials of this procedure would yield the Monte Carlo estimate of the sampling distribution of the vote bias estimator in this situation.

We use this Monte Carlo estimate of the sampling distribution to understand the behavior of the vote bias estimator by calculating its mean, standard deviation, bias (pseudo-population value – mean of the estimates), and skewness and kurtosis coefficients, conducting a normality test and examining its distribution graphically. These characteristics for a 10,000-trial experiment are displayed in Table 4.2 and Figure 4.1. Clearly, Jackman's estimator performs very well in this experiment. The bias of the statistic is very small, at less than one fifth of its standard error, and this standard error is itself very small in relation to the value of the estimator. This suggests that this is a very efficient and perhaps unbiased estimator of the population parameter. This is important in the specific data example under consideration because the point estimate from the U.S. House data is .52, which is not far from the logical null value of .50. Without the knowledge that the variability of this statistic is very small, we would not likely make the judgment that this estimate indicates a nonzero bias in the system. Figure 4.1 displays a histogram of the vote bias estimates, showing right skew and leptokurtosis (note the superimposed normal distribution) and a tight distribution around the mean, characteristics all indicated in Table 4.2. This experimental output therefore gives us a good feel for how this estimator would behave in samples from the real population. The following GAUSS code will execute this vote bias experiment:

```
/*Set parameters*/
n = 29;                    /*set sample size*/
mc_trials = 10000;         /*set number of trials*/
```

TABLE 4.2

Monte Carlo Estimates of the Characteristics of the
Sampling Distribution of the Vote Bias Estimator in Figure 4.1

Mean	.5210
Standard deviation	.007
Bias	−.001
Skewness	.8295
Kurtosis	4.7199
Minimum	.5007
Maximum	.5757
Jarque-Bera test statistic	2,379.29*

NOTE: Monte Carlo experiment: average R^2 = .75, pseudo-population vote bias = .5196, number of trials = 10,000, time elapsed = 1.40 minutes on an IBM clone with a Pentium 133 processor.
*p(vote bias ~ N) < .01.

```
log_beta = -.152; rho = 1.942;
                    /*set pseudo-population parameters*/

/*Calculate the pseudo-population bias estimate*/
pop_bias = (exp(( -1 * log_beta)/rho))/(1 +
    (exp(( -1 * log_beta)/rho)));
w = 1;                /*set error weight*/
index = 1;            /*initialize trial index*/
bias_mc = zeros(mc_trials,1);
                    /*set up empty vector for bias estimates*/
r2_mc = zeros(mc_trials,1);
```
                    /*set up empty vector fo trial R^2's*/
```
do until index > mc_trials;
                    /*start the MC loop*/
  repvote =
    (rndn(n,1) * .0326) + .4566;
                    /*simulate Republican vote*/
  demvote =
    (rndn(n,1) * .0304) + .5281;
                    /*simulate Democratic vote*/
vote_rat =
    ln(repvote./demvote);
                    /*set the X variable*/
err = log(rndn(n,1) + 10);
```
                    /*set error term, adding 10 to allow for logs*/

70

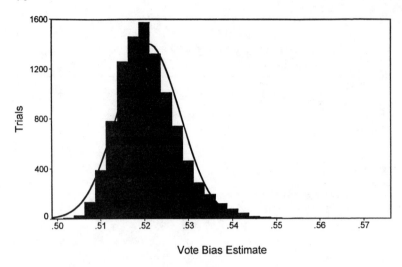

Figure 4.1. Histogram of Vote Bias Estimator

```
err = err -ln(10);              /*incorporate the error weighting
  err = err * w;                constant*/
y = log_beta +
    (rho * vote_rat) + err;
                                /*simulate the dependent variable*/
```

```
/*Regress the simulated y on x*/
screen off;                     /*switch off excess regression output*/
output off;
{vnam,m,slopes,stb,vc,stderr,sigma,cx,r2,resid,
    dwstat}
    = ols(0,y,vote_rat);/*regress y on vote_rat*/
screen on;
  output on;
```

```
/*Calculate and place the bias estimate in the MC vector*/
bias_mc[index,1] = (exp(
    -1*slopes[1,1]/slopes[2,1]))/
    (1 + (exp( -1 * slopes[1,1]/slopes[2,1])));
```

/*Save the R-squared from each trial to assess the congruence of the
    simulation with data*/

```
r2_mc[index,1] = r2;
  index = index + 1;        /*increment trial index*/
endo;                       /*end the trials*/.
```

We can also use this Monte Carlo simulation to make statements about the population value of vote bias in a method analogous to conducting a hypothesis test. Recall that a classic hypothesis test assesses the probability of getting a specific value for a statistic in the data given that the population value of the parameter has some null value. We can make this assessment in a Monte Carlo experiment by setting the pseudo-population value of the parameter in question to the null value and calculating the percentage of trials the estimate of that parameter is above/below the value of the estimate observed in the real data. This is an estimate of the probability of observing the estimate we actually observed in the data, given the pseudo-population. Of course, this procedure requires the assumption that *everything else* besides the null parameter in the pseudo-population is just as it is in the true population. To best approximate this condition, as little change as possible in the original simulation setup should be made, ideally with only a change in the value of the parameter of interest.

To do this in the vote bias simulation, we need to set the pseudo-population value of the parameter to .50 because we want to know whether the minority party needed to get more than 50% of the vote to win 50% of the seats in a House election. The least disruptive way in which to do this is to change the value of the $\log(\hat{\beta})$ parameter in Table 4.1 from −.152 to .000. The test value against which to assess vote bias is .52, the estimated value in the U.S. House data. The question to be addressed is, What is the proportion of the estimates that are greater than .52 given the pseudo-population value of .50? This procedure can be executed with the preceding GAUSS code first by changing the value of $\log(\hat{\beta})$ to .000 and then by including the following lines to assess the proportion of trials in which .52 was exceeded:

```
too_high = bias_mc.>52;  /*too_high is a (t × 1) vector whose
                            cases are 0 or 1 depending on
                            whether or not this condition is met*/
prop = sumc(too_high)/mc_trials;
                         /*prop = proportion of trials in
                            which bias_mc exceeded .52*/
```

A 10,000-trial experiment using this procedure produced only 34 trials in which the observed value of vote bias from this null pseudo-population was greater than the vote bias observed in the U.S. House data. That is, the estimated level of Type I error, $\hat{\alpha}$, for rejecting this null is .0034. Because this $\hat{\alpha}$ is smaller than any conventionally acceptable social science α level, we can reject the null hypothesis that vote bias = .50. It is therefore very likely that there was bias in the electoral system in the United States in this period, assuming that the rest of the pseudo-population model was an accurate reflection of the system at that time. This final caveat, as important in making parametric inferences as it is in conducting Monte Carlo simulation, would need to be verified using substantive theory and perhaps further corroborating evidence.

This Monte Carlo hypothesis test demonstrates the importance of understanding what is assumed in a test and how errors can be made if it is executed incorrectly. One might be tempted to assess the hypothesis that vote bias = .50 by calculating the percentage of cases with vote bias < .50 given a pseudo-population vote bias = .52. This is *backward* in that it estimates the probability of a true value of .52 yielding an observed value of .50. Although the results of the backward and the correct tests are asymptotically equivalent for *symmetrically* distributed statistics, when a statistic is skewed, as the vote bias estimator appears to be, the results of the former will be incorrect. This is because the critical region in the correct approach lies in the thin right-hand tail, whereas the critical region in the backward approach is in the truncated left-hand tail. Therefore, null and observed values the same distance apart will yield different estimated probabilities depending on which side of the distribution the critical region lies.

4.2 Testing a Null Hypothesis Under a Variety of Plausible Conditions

A researcher may wish to test a null hypothesis using Monte Carlo simulation, as in Section 4.1, but may not be certain how to characterize the underlying pseudo-population. For example, we might want to use Lijphart and Crepaz's (1991) index of government corporatism to test whether the United States, with a score of −1.341, is less corporatist than average. Even if this question could be conceptualized so as to use a parametric statistical test, it probably is not appropriate given that the variable is nonnormal (based on theoretical considerations and the observed data) and the sample size is only 18 (Lijphart and Crepaz evaluate only major industrialized nations). If we knew the underlying distribution of the variable, then it would be an easy matter to proceed, as in Section 4.1, but what can be done when we are not confident in our knowledge of this distribution?

When it is not possible to be certain that a specific distribution has generated a variable, we may be able to specify a *range* of distributions that could plausibly have done so. We then can run a *series of experiments* using these distributions in the pseudo-populations, evaluating the null hypothesis for each experiment. The results of these experiments then can be used to make some judgment about the likelihood of the null hypothesis being true in the population.

As an example of this process, I conducted 78 experiments using various distributions to test the plausibility that the United States is less corporatist than the average industrialized nation, using the Lijphart and Crepaz index. In each experiment, the question was, What is the proportion of generated cases that are less than -1.341 on a standardized scale, given a null hypothesis pseudo-population with a mean of 0? This proportion is an estimate of the probability of getting the score we observed for the United States had the country really had an underlying score of 0, the overall average. That is, this proportion is an estimate of the Type I error rate (α) of rejecting the null incorrectly, $\hat{\alpha}$. Using social science conventions about α, we then can make a judgment about the null hypothesis in the population.

I used a series of beta distributions to generate my pseudo-corporatism data. Varying the *a* and *b* parameters independently from 1 to 30 led to the pseudo-population distributions of the variable, *x*, from a uniform distribution to an approximately normal distribution and to ones that had high levels of both positive and negative skew. Given our lack of knowledge of the underlying population generating function, this wide range of distributions is appropriate. The following GAUSS code generated some of these experiments, incrementing the *a* parameter from 30 to 1.01 while holding *b* at 30:

```
/*Set parameters*/
n = 10000;                      /*set sample size*/
orig_a = 30; orig_b = 30;
a = orig_a; b = orig_b;  /*set beta parameters*/
test_val = -1.341;              /*set value of the test statistic to be
                                  assessed*/
expers = 15;                    /*set number of experiments to be
                                  run; must be > 1*/

/*Set necessary quantities*/
exp_num = 1;                    /*set index for experiments*/
```

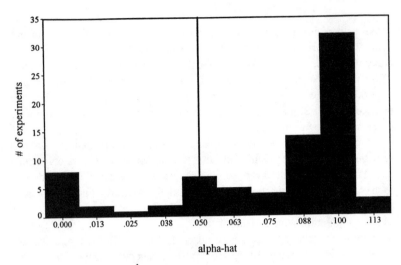

alpha-hat

Figure 4.2. Histogram of $\hat{\alpha}$ for Corporatism Experiments

```
output = zeros(expers,6);
                        /*set up empty vector for experiment results*/
do until exp_num > expers;
                        /*start the experiments loop*/
x =bet(a,b,n);          /*generate a beta distributed x variable*/

/*Standardize x to mean = 0 and sd = 1*/
 x = (x - (a/(a + b)))/(sqrt((a * b)/((a + b)^2
    * (a + b + 1)))));

/*Calculate and store output from experiment*/
  dummy = x. < test_val;
                        /*for each case, set dummy to1 if x l test_val*/
  output[exp_num,1] =
   sumc(dummy)/n;      /*set first column to the proportion of x
                            < test_val*/
  output[exp_num,2] = a;
                        /*set second column to a value for the
                          experiment*/
  output[exp_num,3] = b;
                        /*set third column to b value for the
                          experiment*/
  {skew,kurt,w,prob_w} =
```

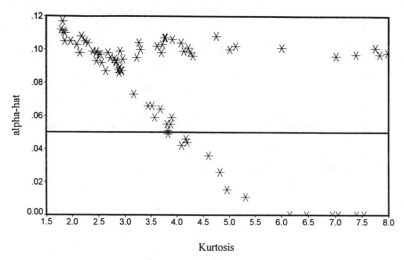

Figure 4.3. Kurtosis Versus $\hat{\alpha}$

```
    jarqbera(x,n);              /*run normality test on x*/
    output[exp_num,4] = skew;   /*set fourth column to
                                   skewness coefficient of x*/
    output[exp_num,5] = kurt;   /*set fifth column to
                                   kurtosis coefficient of x*/
    output[exp_num,6] = prob_w; /*set sixth column to
                                   probability of x being
                                   normal*/
    exp_num = exp_num + 1;      /*increment exp_num*/

/*Increment a*/
a = a - ((orig_a)/(expers - 1));
if a <= 1;                      /*loop to assure a > 1*/
a = 1.01; c
endif;
endo;                           /*stop the experiments
                                   loop*/.
```

Figure 4.2 shows that $\hat{\alpha}$ was greater than .05 for most of the experiments. Using a conventional acceptable α level of .05, then, this leads to the conclusion that under most plausible population distributions for corporatism, the null hypothesis that the United States is not different from the average industrialized country cannot be rejected.

76

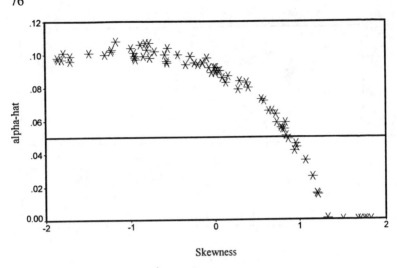

Figure 4.4. Skewness Versus $\hat{\alpha}$

On the other hand, Figure 4.2 also shows that there were several experiments that had very small $\hat{\alpha}$'s, suggesting that under certain conditions the null may not be true. We must then ask ourselves, What might these conditions be, and could they plausibly exist in the real world? Two characteristics on which the pseudo-populations varied considerably across experiments were the kurtosis and the skewness of the variable. By saving the estimated skewness and kurtosis coefficients for each experiment, we can see whether or not these characteristics are associated with $\hat{\alpha}$. Figure 4.3 plots the kurtosis of an experiment's x variable versus its $\hat{\alpha}$. The reference line on the y axis shows the conventional α, .05. An interesting pattern emerges in this plot. Between kurtosis values of 1.8 (a uniform distribution) and 3.0 (a normal distribution, if symmetric), kurtosis has little effect on $\hat{\alpha}$ and all of these experiments are well above the .05 level. But as the variable becomes leptokurtic, the experiments branch off in two distinct directions. The upper group continues to yield an $\hat{\alpha}$ level in the .10 range, but the lower group heads down quickly, ending up with $\hat{\alpha}$'s of as low as .00 by a kurtosis level of 6.0. Why would some of these experiments be affected by kurtosis and some not? The answer lies in the experimental design and the skewness of the variable.

In the beta distribution, kurtosis and skewness are related through a common dependence on a and b (Table 2.3). The higher the absolute value of the skewness of a beta distributed variable, the higher the kurtosis, although the reverse is not necessarily true (e.g., it is possible to have a symmetric beta distributed variable with high or low kurtosis). Therefore, it may be the skewness of the variable that is causing the odd pattern seen in Figure 4.3. Figure 4.4 plots $\hat{\alpha}$ against the skewness of the generated variable and indicates that this is in fact the case. Skewness has a strong effect on $\hat{\alpha}$, but only when it is positive. The short, thick left-hand tail of a positively skewed distribution appears to greatly reduce the chances of x being less than −1.341, which makes sense intuitively. By the time the skewness coefficient of the generated variable reaches 1.0, $\hat{\alpha}$ is less than .05. The odd pattern in Figure 4.3 is therefore the result of some of the highly kurtotic experiments being very negatively skewed (the upper group) and some of them being very positively skewed (the bottom group).

The substantive interpretation of these experiments is therefore conditional. If the underlying corporatist variable has a skewness coefficient of less than 1.0, then we cannot reject the null hypothesis of no difference from average for the United States at the .05 α level. However, we could confidently reject this null if the variable has any other unimodal distribution. The question then becomes one of how likely it is that the corporatist variable actually is distributed in this fashion, and this can only be answered through theory and/or a further examination of real-world data.

An important problem with this approach to inference, however, is that we never know the exact α level of our test. In parametric hypothesis testing, if all the assumptions of the procedure hold, then we can set the rate of Type I error by specifying α in the testing procedure. But by assessing the substantive null hypothesis with a variety of statistical null hypotheses, the best we can say is that the probability of Type I error is *at least* a certain level or *at most* a certain level, and this is only when the null is rejected or not rejected in all experiments. If we have a situation, as in Figures 4.2 and 4.3, where under some conditions the null is rejected and under some conditions it is not, then we cannot even say this much. On the other hand, it usually is better to draw conditional and limited conclusions with strong evidentiary support than to draw exact and general conclusions that are based on erroneous assumptions.

4.3 Assessing the Quality of an Inference Method

In conducting statistical inference, we are concerned with two types of error: Type I error, rejecting a true null hypothesis, and Type II error, failing to reject a false null hypothesis. Except in certain special cases where analytical mathematics can be used, to evaluate these error rates in a test, one needs to know the true value of the population parameter being tested. Given that we conduct inferential tests because we do *not* know the value of that parameter, inferential errors never can be identified by looking only at real-world data. Monte Carlo simulation is the only general way in which to make these assessments because with it we have information about the value of the population parameters involved (Davidson & MacKinnon, 1993, p. 768).

Many situations may arise in which a researcher would need to estimate an inference method's error rate. Type I error rates are known for parametric inference tests if all the assumptions of the test are met, but this probably is an exceptional situation. What about the Type I error rate of parametric inference when the model's assumptions are violated? And what about the Type II error rate of a test? What about the Type I and II error rates of tests for statistics that have no strong parametric theory behind them? In Section 4.4, I discuss estimating the Type I error rate of a parametric test when its assumptions do not hold. Here I demonstrate estimating error rates of tests for which parametric theory is weak or nonexistent.

The basic logic behind estimating the Type I error rate of an inferential test derives in a straightforward manner from the definition of a Type I error:

1. Generate a pseudo-sample from a pseudo-population in which the null hypothesis is *true*.
2. Estimate the model.
3. Conduct the inferential test, setting the nominal α level as desired.
4. Assess whether a Type I error has been committed (i.e., Has the true null been rejected?).
5. Repeat for t trials.

The $\hat{\alpha}$ of the test is then the proportion of trials for which the null was (incorrectly) rejected.

To estimate the Type II error rate of a test, we conduct a similar procedure but with one important difference (e.g., Duval & Groeneveld, 1987). Because a Type II error occurs when we incorrectly fail to reject a false null hypothesis, the null hypothesis must in fact be false in the pseudo-population:

1. Generate a pseudo-sample from a pseudo-population in which the null hypothesis is *false*.
2. Estimate the model.
3. Conduct the inferential test, setting the nominal α level as desired.
4. Assess whether a Type II error has been committed (i.e., Has the false null not been rejected?).
5. Repeat for t trials.

The estimated Type II error rate of the test is the proportion of trials for which the false null was (incorrectly) not rejected.

When assessing Type II error rate, it is important to consider the relative difference between the population and null values with respect to the standard deviation of the estimated statistic. This is because a test will have a lower Type II error rate the further apart the null and the true parameter values are, regardless of the distribution of the statistic. This is not the case for Type I error rate estimation because in that case the null can only take on a single value—that of the parameter in the population.

Consider the assessment of the error rates of a bootstrap percentile confidence interval around an OLS regression coefficient when the error is highly skewed and the sample is small (Mooney, 1996).[16] With nonnormal error and small sample, we certainly cannot use parametric inference with confidence, but the bootstrap percentile confidence interval's performance also has been called into question in such a situation (Efron, 1987; Schenker, 1985). For both tests, the asymptotic theory assuring the accuracy of the nominal α level cannot be invoked in small samples, and the standard power analyses used to estimate Type II error rates also are not applicable.

I ran a Monte Carlo simulation to estimate the error rates of this interval, setting the nominal α level at .05, the sample size at 25, the independent variable, x, to the integers 1 to 25, and the error term to have a standardized chi-square distribution with 1 degree of freedom.[17] The pseudo-population value of the model's constant term was set at 1.0, and the slope value was set at 2.0. The average R^2 of the 1,000 trials[18] was .55. Type I error rate estimation was done by testing whether the true slope value (2.0) was excluded from the bootstrap confidence interval for each trial; Type II error rate assessment was done by checking whether a reasonable but false null hypothesis (slope = 0.0) was included in the interval. In this way, both Type I and II errors were estimated using the same pseudo-population. For each trial in which an error was committed, a counter variable for that type of error was increased by 1 and the proportions of error were calculated by dividing the final value of each counter by the total number of trials. The following GAUSS code undertakes this procedure:

```
n = 25;              /*set sample size*/
b = 1000;            /*set number of bootstrap replications*/
mctrials = 1000;     /*set number of Monte Carlo trials*/
df = 1;              /*set for degrees of freedom for the χ²
                     distributed error term*/
w = 15;              /*set error weight*/
```

```
nbeta = 0;                /*set the false null value of the test for
                           Type II error rate estimation*/
nom_alpha = .05;          /*set the nominal alpha level for the test*/
tbeta = 2.0; tcons = 1.0;
                          /*set pseudo-population parameters*/
t = 1;                    /*set trial index*/

/*Define Monte Carlo output vectors/scalars*/
mc_r2 = zeros(mctrials,1);
                          /*set up empty R² vector*/
TypeI = 0;                /*Type I error counter*/
TypeII = 0;               /*Type II error counter*/

/*Monte Carlo generation of data*/
do while t <= mctrials;
    b11 = zeros(b,1);/*used in bootstrapping*/
    i = 1;
    x = seqa(1,1,N);  /*define the x variable*/
    err = chi(df,n);
    err = (sumc(err) 2D df)
      /sqrt(2 * df);   /*define the error as a standardized
                        chi-square(df)*/
    y = (tbeta * x) +
    tcons + (err * w);/*define the pseudo-population*/

/*Regress full sample Y on X and save residuals for resamples*/
    _output = 0;         /*order OLS procedure not to print
                          statistics*/
    _olsres = 1;         /*order OLS procedure to calculate
                          residuals*/
  {v,m,bet,s,v,se,sig,cx,r2,resid,dw} =
    ols(0,y,x);
  mc_r2[t,1] = r2;       /*save R² for evaluation of the
                          experiment*/

/*Resample residuals for bootstrap confidence interval*/
  index = seqa(1,1,n);
  do while i <= b;
  re = submat(resid,ceil(rndu(n,1) * n)',0);
  yr = bet[1,1] + (x * bet[2,1]) + re;
```

```
   {v,m,bsb2,s,v,se,sig,cx,r2,res,dw} =
                                   ols(0,yr,x);
   b11[i,1] = bsb2[2,.];     /*save the resampled data's
                               OLS slope*/
   i = i + 1;
   endo;                     /*end of resampling loop*/
 b11 = sortc(b11,1);         /*sort bootstrapped slopes for CI
                               construction*/
```

/*Define the percentile points for *B* at alpha = nom_alpha*/
```
   ll = ceil((b * nom_alpha)/2);
   ul = ceil((b - ll) + 1);
```

/*Loop for computing Type I and II errors for the percentile CI*/
```
   if tbeta <= b11[ll] or
      tbeta >= b11[ul];       /*if the slope estimate is outside
                                the CI*/
   TypeI = TypeI + 1;
   endif;
   if nbeta >= b11[ll] and
      nbeta <= b11[ul];       /*if the null slope value is inside
                                the CI*/
   TypeII = TypeII + 1;
   endif;
   t = t + 1;                 /*increment the trial counter*/
 endo;
```

/*Estimate the error rates by dividing the counters by the number of trials*/
```
TypeI = TypeI/mctrials; TypeII = TypeII/mctrials;
```

An important consideration in error rate estimation is the standard by which to evaluate these estimates. The standard for Type II error rate evaluation is straightforward. A Type II error rate is better than a competing Type II error rate if it is less than its competitor. That is, less Type II error always is better, other things being equal, and the standard is a comparative one; it is assessed in relation to a competing test's Type II error rate or that of the same test under different statistical conditions.

By contrast, there is an absolute standard for Type I error estimation: the nominal α level of the test. The idea is that the test should have the level of Type I error that is specified for it at the outset. If the rate is too high, then more Type I errors are made than were agreed to be acceptable. If the rate is lower than the nominal α, then more Type II errors than necessary are made given an acceptable Type I error rate. This is because Type I and Type II error rates are inversely, if not linearly, related. Therefore, we say that an inferential test is *accurate* to the extent that its true Type I error rate (as estimated in the Monte Carlo experiment) is equal to the nominal Type I error rate specified at the outset of the test (Hall, 1992, p. 12). In the case of Type II error, we say that a test is *preferred* compared to some competitor test if its estimated Type II error rate is less than the competitor's rate.

In the experiment just described, the estimated Type II error rate was .02, meaning that in 20 of the 1,000 trials the false null of a 0 slope was included in the confidence interval. Because there was no other test being evaluated in this experiment, we cannot make any comparative judgments, but there appears to be only a small chance of making a Type II error here. But note that this error rate would increase if the false null was closer to the true slope value. A comparison of just how quickly the Type II error rate increases in this way could be undertaken using a series of simulation experiments.

The Type I error rate of this test is estimated to be .067 because in 67 of the 1,000 trials the true parameter value was excluded from the bootstrap percentile confidence interval. This means that, using this confidence interval in this situation, we would commit 34% more Type I errors than we had held to be acceptable by setting the nominal α level at .05. Whether or not this incongruity means that this confidence interval procedure should not be used under these conditions depends on a researcher's judgment.

In practice, a researcher faced with such a situation could proceed as follows. First, he or she would conduct the inferential test and report the findings from the actual data. Then, simulation experiments estimating the Type I and II error rates of the test would be conducted. These experimental results then would be reported along with the real data results, giving the reader all the information available with which to judge the findings.

4.4 Assessing the Robustness of Parametric Inference to Assumption Violations

Sometimes a researcher wants to use parametric inference but is not certain whether it is appropriate in the statistical situation at hand. For instance, he or she may be using OLS regression on a sample of 35 cases with a highly skewed dependent variable. In such a case, it is unclear whether the slope estimates will be distributed normally. Therefore, the researcher may want to evaluate the standard parametric test's error rate under a variety of conditions that approximate his or her data. For example, he or she might simulate pseudo-populations with a range of sample sizes and distributions of the dependent variable and evaluate how the Type I error rate behaves across them, combining the procedures discussed in Sections 4.2 and 4.3.

Given the frequency with which the assumptions of statistical tests in the social sciences are suspected to be violated, this could be a widely useful application of Monte Carlo simulation. The small sample behavior of statistical tests is an area of particular interest because theoretical substantiation for most parametric inference techniques is based on large sample theory (e.g., Cicchitelli, 1989; Everitt, 1979; Hendry & Harrison, 1974).

Because there may be several dimensions of the statistical situation that could affect the error rate, the researcher needs to consider his or her experimental design carefully. In the OLS regression example, we might want to assess the independent effects of variations in sample size, skewness and kurtosis of the dependent variable and/or error term, correlation among the independent variables, R^2, and so forth. The more complicated the model, the more characteristics may have an effect. The experimenter needs to define the relevant and realistic range of each of these characteristics and vary them systematically and independently across these ranges in his or her experiments. The following steps would be followed to undertake such a set of experiments:

1. Conduct a Monte Carlo experiment on an inferential test with a given pseudo-population, estimating the Type I error rate of the test, $\hat{\alpha}$.
2. Save $\hat{\alpha}$ and the relevant characteristics of the pseudo-population in a row of a matrix.
3. Independently and systematically vary the characteristic(s) of the pseudo-population and conduct Steps 1 and 2 again.
4. Repeat Step 3 until the desired range of each of the relevant characteristics of the pseudo-population has been represented in the experiments.
5. Use RSA to estimate the independent effects of the characteristics of the pseudo-population on $\hat{\alpha}$.

Consider assessing the impact of sample size and error term skew on the Type I error rate of a parametric t test on a bivariate OLS regression slope. The standard OLS results assure us that this test will be accurate with a "large" sample or if the error term is normally distributed. But there are many situations in the social sciences that do not meet these conditions, such as if one were to use the Lijphart and Crepaz (1991) corporatism index as the dependent variable in a regression model (as they do). I evaluated the performance of this test with a series of Monte Carlo experiments that varied independently in sample size (from 10 to 50 by fives) and in error term skewness. The latter was done by using a standardized χ^2 distribution for the error, varying the degrees of freedom from 1 to 17 by ones across experiments. That is, I ran 17 experiments with a sample size of 10, 17 with a sample size of 15, and so forth, using each of the distributions of the error term at each sample size, resulting in 153 experiments. The other characteristics of these experiments were held constant throughout; the constant and slope of the pseudo-populations were set at 1.0 and 2.0, respectively, the average R^2 of the experiments was .55, and x was the set of integers from 1 to n. The following GAUSS code conducted all these experiments in a single run of 15.04 minutes on an IBM clone with a Pentium 133 in DOS:

```
/*Set up experiment parameters*/
max_n = 50; min_n = 10;
                /*set the range of n*/
step_n = 5;     /*step to increment sample size between
                experiments; must go into the range of n evenly*/
n = min_n;      /*set initial sample size*/
max_df = 17; min_df = 1;
                /*set the range of error term df*/
step_df = 1;    /*step to increment df between experiments;
                must go into the range of df evenly*/
df = min_df;    /*set initial for χ² distributed error term*/
mctrials = 1000;
                /*set number of Monte Carlo trials per experiment*/
e_weight = 15;/*set error weight*/
exp_n = (((max_n - min_n)/
step_n) + 1) * (((max_df -
min_df)/step_df) + 1);
                /*set number of experiments*/
tbeta = 2.0; tcons = 1.0;
                /*set the pseudo-population parameters*/
nom_alph = .05;/*set nominal rate of Type I error*/

/*Initialize experiment output vectors*/
ex_type1 = zeros(exp_n,1);
```

```
ex_r2 = zeros(exp_n,1);
ex_df = zeros(exp_n,1);
ex_n = zeros(exp_n,1);
ex_skew = zeros(exp_n,1);
results = zeros(exp_n,5);
```

```
/*Start the experiments loop*/
   do while exp_n >= 1;
   type1 = 0;     /*initialize Type I error counter for this experiment*/
   t = 1;         /*initialize trial counter for this experiment*/
   mc_r2 = zeros(mctrials,1);
                  /*initialize R-squared vector for this experiment*/
mc_skew = zeros(mctrials,1);
                  /*initialize skew vector for this experiment*/
```

/*Define the two-tailed t score for alpha = nom_alpha with $df = n - 2$ for
     the t test*/
```
   tcal = 1.5; tdf = n 2D 2; p = .5;
   do until p <= (nom_alph/2);
     p = cdftc(tcal,tdf);
     tcal = tcal + .01;
   endo;
   tcal = tcal - 0.01;
```

```
/*Monte Carlo data generation*/
   do while t <= mctrials;
     x = seqa(1,1,N);
     err = chi(df,n);
     err = (sumc(err) - df)/
     sqrt(2 * df);
                  /*yield standardized χ²(df) distributederror*/
```

```
   /*Define the pseudo-population model*/
   y = (tbeta * x) + tcons + (err * e_weight);
```

```
   /*Conduct the OLS regression analysis*/
   _output = 0;/*order OLS procedure not to print statistics*/
   _olsres = 1;/*order OLS procedure to calculate residuals*/
   {v,m,bet,s,v,se,sig,cx,r2,resid,dw}
     = ols(0,y,x);
                  /*regress y on x*/
```

```
    mc_r2[t,1] = r2;
                    /*save this trial's R-squared*/
    /*Assess Type I error for two-tailed t test*/
    if tbeta <= (bet[2,1] - (tcal * se[2,1])) or
    tbeta >= (bet[2,1] + (tcal * se[2,1]));
      type1 = type1 + 1;
    endif;
```

/*Calculate and save the skewness coefficient of residuals*/
```
    {skew,kurt,test,p_test}=jarqbera(resid,n);
    mc_skew[t,1] = skew;
  t = t + 1;      /*increment the trial counter for this experiment*/
endo;                   /*end a single experiment after t trials*/
type1 = type1/mctrials;
                    /*calculate the proportion of Type I errors for this
                    experiment*/
```

/*Place experiment output into vectors*/
```
ex_type1[exp_n,1] = type1;
ex_r2[exp_n,1] = meanc(mc_r2);
ex_df[exp_n,1] = df;
ex_n[exp_n,1] = n;
ex_skew[exp_n,1] = meanc(skew);
```

/*Increment parameters for the next experiment*/
```
if n < max_n;
   n = n + step_n;
   e_weight = e_weight;
                    /*could increment error weight by addition*/
   else;
   df = df + step_df;
   n = min_n;
endif;
print "End of experiment number:" exp_n;
exp_n = exp_n - 1;/*index experiments loop*/
endo;                   /*end multiple experiments loop*/
```

/*Set up and print output matrix to outfile*/
```
format /m1 /ldn 10,3;
print "Output matrix columns: Type I
    rate,R2,df,n,skew";
```

```
/*Horizontally concatenate output vectors*/
results = ex_type1~ex_r2~ex_df~ex_n~ex_skew;
print results;
```

Note two important points about the preceding code. First, consider the section headed "/*Increment parameters for the next experiment*/." The goal here is to cycle through all potential values for the degrees of freedom of the error term (*df*) and sample size (*n*) independently. This is done with an "if/else" structure, which first increments *n* to its preset maximum (*max_n*) holding *df* constant, then increments *df* one step and runs through the samples sizes again, and so forth. The program ends when the desired number of experiments is reached (*exp_n*), where *exp_n* is set to be a function of the ranges of *n* and *df* to be represented in the experiments. This procedure allows a large number of experiments to be run in a systematic fashion in a single program and will aggregate the output conveniently. An important practical point here is that an experimenter should try out various values of the parameters to be used in short runs to be certain that they are incrementing as desired.

The second programming point involves the section headed "/*Define the two-tailed *t* score for alpha = nom_alpha with $df = n - 2$ for the *t* test*/." Here the appropriate *t* score for the test (tcal) is calculated with an iteration technique. This is done, first, because the critical *t* score varies with sample size and, second, because GAUSS does not automatically return *t* scores given degrees of freedom and probability values, as would be convenient. It is therefore necessary to "trick" the program into giving the *t* score needed by using the command that returns the probability value given a *t* score and a degrees-of-freedom value.[19]

In my OLS example, I used each of the 153 experiments as a case of data in an RSA to explore the factors that influenced the Type I error rate of this test. An important consideration in conducting RSA is what the dependent variable should be. Because I am interested in how closely $\hat{\alpha}$ comes to the nominal α, one choice for a dependent variable would be the difference between $\hat{\alpha}$ and α in an experiment. However, I am not concerned with whether this value is positive or negative because I do not care whether the test makes more or fewer errors than are nominally allowed.[20] Therefore, I use the absolute value of the difference between $\hat{\alpha}$ and α as the dependent variable for the RSA. Multiplying this value by −1 allows the resulting coefficients of the RSA to be assessed in a straightforward manner in terms of the direction of their impact on the performance of the test because a positive coefficient indicates a positive effect on performance.

TABLE 4.3

Response Surface Analysis Assessing the Effect of Error Skew and
Sample Size on a Parametric t Test for an OLS Regression Slope

Independent Variable	OLS Slope Estimate
|Error term skew|	.0035*
	(.002)
(Error term skew)^2	−.0040**
	(.001)
(Sample size)*(Error term skew)^2	.00005**
	(.0000)
Constant	−.0065**
	(.001)

NOTES: OLS = ordinary least squares, $N = 153$, $R_a^2 = .25$. OLS regression analysis: dependent variable (performance) $= -1*|\alpha - [\hat{\alpha}]|$, where $\alpha = .05$, unit of analysis = a Monte Carlo experiment. Monte Carlo experiments: $X = (1, 2, 3, \ldots, n)$, range of $n = 10$ to 50 by fives, range of error skew = −1.46 to 2.64, number of trials = 1,000.
*$p(\beta = 0) < .01$, **$p(\beta = 0) < .001$.

My final RSA model was estimated using OLS, with the selection of the independent variables being based on theoretical considerations and the results of multiple estimations (Box & Draper, 1987). For example, the fit of the model in each experiment (as measured by the average R^2) had no discernible impact on the test's performance and so was left out of the final RSA model. The skew of the error term was quadratically related to performance, as was sample size when interacted with the square of the error skew (Table 4.3).[21] This all makes theoretical sense in that as we move away from violating the assumptions of this parametric test (i.e., as skew in the error decreases and/or n increases), the test performs better. Figure 4.5 displays this relationship graphically using the fitted response surface. For fairly large samples ($n > 40$), high levels of error skew do not affect test performance; however, in small samples, high levels of skew can lead to poor performance. What these results mean for the use of this test for a researcher undertaking real data analysis depends on the size of his or her sample and the skew of his or her error term.

4.5 Comparing Estimators' Properties

A researcher sometimes may have a choice between two or more estimators of the same population parameter. For example, in estimating the central tendency of a variable, he or she might need to choose among the mean, median, and trimmed mean with a variety of trimming proportions.

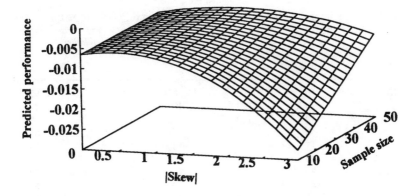

Figure 4.5. Predicted Confidence Interval Performance Versus Error Skew and Sample Size

Sometimes analytical statistical theory can be used to make the choice. For example, we know that the median is less efficient than the mean. But sometimes statistical theory does not provide clear comparative evaluations. For example, what level of trim should be used for a trimmed mean if efficiency or unbiasedness is of greatest concern? A common situation in which this sort of question can arise is in small sample problems because much statistical theory is based on large sample proof.

Monte Carlo simulation can be used to compare estimators empirically in such a situation. The basic idea is to evaluate the estimators on the same criteria in identical simulated situations using the principles laid out in the previous sections. First, the researcher determines his or her criterion for comparison, perhaps the mean-squared error, and defines a pseudo-population that resembles the population of interest. Next, he or she applies the estimators to be compared to the same data generated from this pseudo-population in a series of trials.[22] Finally, the evaluative criterion is calculated for each estimator across the trials, and comparisons are made between estimators. If possible, a range of such experiments should be undertaken, varying the pseudo-population in ways relevant to the question at hand.

Beck and Katz (1995) undertake a series of experiments to compare, among other things, the relative efficiency of OLS slope estimators, and Parks (1967) corrected slope estimators for pooled cross-sectional data exhibiting autocorrelation and heteroskedasticity. Mathematical analysis

TABLE 4.4

Relative Efficiency of Ordinary Least Squares and Parks Slope Estimates

		Contemporaneous Error Correlation			
N^a	t^b	.00	.25	.50	.75
10	10	102	100	99	97
	20	109	101	88	72
	30	112	105	90	68
	40	109	101	87	66
15	15	101	100	99	98
	20	108	102	93	84
	30	111	101	88	72
	40	111	100	83	64
20	20	102	101	100	99
	25	107	102	97	90
	30	107	100	91	80
	40	112	104	92	76

SOURCE: Beck and Katz (1995, p. 642). Reprinted with permission of American Political Science Association.
NOTE: Relative efficiency of more than 100 indicates the superiority of ordinary least squares.
a. Number of cross-sectional units per time point.
b. Number of time points.

here is intractable in instances where there are few cases per time period and few time periods, a common circumstance in political science data. Beck and Katz's (1995, p. 639) relative efficiency criterion is the ratio of one root mean-square error to the other, multiplied by 100 to convert it to a percentage:

$$\text{Relative Efficiency} = 100 * \frac{\sqrt{\sum_{t=1}^{1000} (\hat{\beta}_P^t - \beta_{MC})^2}}{\sqrt{\sum_{t=1}^{1000} (\hat{\beta}_{OLS}^t - \beta_{MC})^2}}, \quad (4.3)$$

where the number of trials is 1,000, β_{MC} is the pseudo-population slope, and $\hat{\beta}_{OLS}$ and $\hat{\beta}_P$ are the OLS and Parks estimates, respectively (Parks, 1967). Because Beck and Katz are interested in how relative efficiency varies with the number of time units, cases per time unit, and correlation among the errors in a given time period, they designed a series of experiments in which these factors varied independently. Table 4.4 displays their results, which indicate that OLS performs as well as or better than Parks when the contemporaneous error correlation is less than .5. This is important because contemporaneous error correlation in their field seldom is as high as .5 (Beck & Katz, 1995, p. 642).

Table 4.4 is a good way in which to summarize the results of Beck and Katz's (1995) 48 experiments, but there is a limit to the number of experimental results that can be displayed clearly this way. Elsewhere, I have compared five inference techniques (four bootstrap methods and parametric inference) as used with OLS regression with skewed error and small samples (Mooney, 1996). I was interested in the differences between these techniques in terms of their performance approximating the nominal α level and conducted 885 Monte Carlo experiments to assess this. With so many factors (test type, sample size, and their interactions) and so many experiments, the simple tabular display of Beck and Katz could not be used. Also, I was interested in conducting statistical tests to assess hypotheses about the performance of these techniques. Therefore, RSA was the appropriate analytic choice, and the results of this analysis are displayed in Table 4.5. The dependent variable is the $\hat{\alpha}$ performance measure discussed in Section 4.4. The tests of comparison were between the parametric approach and each of the bootstrap tests. This was done by including dummy variables for each of the bootstrap tests in the RSA and using the parametric test as the reference category. That is, each case was an experiment in which one of the five tests was used. That test's dummy would equal 1 for that case, and all the other dummies would equal 0. Therefore, a test that the dummy's coefficient was 0 would be a test that that technique had better α-level performance than the parametric test. I also included in the RSA the natural log of an experiment's sample size and interactions of this with the test dummies to assess the nonlinear effect of sample size.

The statistically significant coefficients for the main and interaction effects of two of the bootstrap tests in the RSA model (Table 4.5) indicate that these tests do indeed outperform the parametric test in these experiments. Perhaps a more intuitive way in which to communicate this result is by plotting the predicted value of the dependent variable for each test against sample size. Figure 4.6 shows how effective such a display can be. Clearly, the percentile t and normal approximation bootstrap methods have superior performance across the range of samples. This graph also shows the nonlinear effect of sample size and how the performance of these tests

TABLE 4.5

Response Surface Analysis of Monte Carlo Experiments on α-Level
Inference Performance Regarding a Bivariate Regression Slope

	Estimated Ordinary Least Squares Coefficient
Normal approximation	.0981*
	(.0084)
BCa	.0082
	(.0098)
Percentile	.0011
	(.0091)
Percentile-t	.1352*
	(.0069)
Normal approximation * ln(sample size)	−.0255*
	(.0024)
Percentile * ln(sample size)	.0001
	(.0026)
BCa * ln(sample size)	−.0011
	(.0028)
Percentile-t * ln(sample size)	−.0354*
	(.0020)
ln(sample size)	.0342*
	(.0019)
Constant	−.1396*
	(.0065)

SOURCE: Mooney (1996). Reprinted with permission of University of Wisconsin Press.
NOTES: $N = 885$, $R_a^2 = .70$, Breusch-Pagan ($df = 9$) = 196.04. Numbers in parentheses are White (1980)
estimated standard errors to account for heteroskedasticity. OLS regression analysis: unit of analysis =
a Monte Carlo experiment, dependent variable = −1 * |α − $\hat{α}$|. Monte Carlo experiments: $X = (1, 2, 3,$
$\ldots, n)$, residuals resampling, trials per experiment = 500, bootstrap resamples = 1,000.
*$p(\beta = 0) < .01$.

tends to be indistinguishable as sample size reaches 40 or so. These aspects
of the experimental results would not be seen easily in either a tabular
display or the RSA output in Table 4.5.

5. CONCLUSION

Monte Carlo simulation is a flexible and powerful tool for social scientists
working with statistical models. This is especially true today, as computer
power and the creative application of statistical theory have combined to

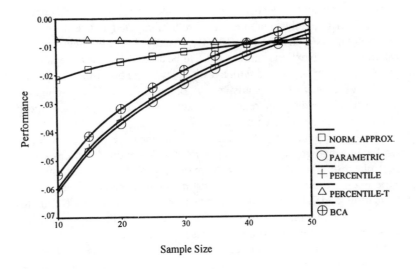

Figure 4.6. Predicted Performance on Type I Error for Ordinary Least Squares
Slope Inference Tests
SOURCE: Mooney (1996), based on 885 Monte Carlo experiments. Reprinted with permission of
University of Wisconsin Press.
NOTE: The closer to 0.00, the better the α-level performance.

make simulation both more feasible and more necessary as we assess the
assumptions of parametric inference in our data and as we apply and
develop new statistical estimators and tests. The applications discussed in
Chapter 4 are only examples of the ways in which this technique can be
used to understand the behavior of statistics and thereby to help understand
social behavior. The limits of Monte Carlo simulation lie only in the limits
of our creativity in applying it to new situations and in our ability to
understand social processes well enough to simulate them.

Monte Carlo simulation can be complicated, however, especially as we
move away from the simple examples used in this monograph to the
simulation of multiequation models with many variables, more complex
estimators, and so forth. Therefore, I conclude with some suggestions on
how to reduce confusion and error in Monte Carlo practice.

Careful planning is crucial to the successful execution of a simulation
experiment. The researcher must systematically think through what he or
she wants to do long before sitting down to write out computer code. First,
this means developing a very deep understanding of both the social process

to be simulated and the statistics to be evaluated. The researcher then must carefully write out the symbolic model to be simulated and define each of the components of that model explicitly, based on his or her deep theoretical knowledge. Next, the characteristic to be assessed needs to be defined. Is the researcher concerned with a test's α level, the bias of a statistic, the relative efficiency of two statistics, or something else? Close thought to this issue will lead to a more efficient experiment, as unimportant aspects of the simulation can be eliminated.

When writing the computer code to conduct the experiment, it is best to work with small groups of code separately. Self-contained sections are the best place to start. For example, in writing a program to run multiple experiments testing the bias of an estimator of a parameter in a multiequation model, begin with the components of one equation. Define the constants and random variables individually, checking the code for each to be sure it is correct. Constants are easy to check; they must return the specific value you have assigned them or else they are incorrect. Random variable generating algorithms are less straightforward to evaluate because, by definition, the output can take on a variety of values. These are best evaluated by generating many thousands of cases (to eliminate any random oddities) and checking the characteristics of that variable against those of the distribution desired. Calculate the range, mean, standard deviation, and skewness and kurtosis coefficients of the generated variable and then compare them to the values that are expected theoretically. Construct a histogram of the variable and compare it to the theoretical PDF. Although random variation undoubtedly will cause at least small discrepancies between the observed and theoretical values even if the algorithm is correct, this procedure will highlight problems that are hard to see in the computer code.

Once you are confident that the individual components of a segment of your program are correct, string them together in natural combinations to see whether they work as expected. For example, run a single equation of a multiequation model to see whether the estimated parameters have the sampling distributions expected of them. Of course, this cannot be done when the statistic has no theoretically understood sampling distribution (which probably is why you are running the simulations in the first place). But in a complex experiment, there usually are many parameters that are not of central interest that can be used to check the performance of the code. For example, one might run a simulation to estimate the sampling distribution of the switch point in a switching regression model, given that there is little theoretical guidance as to this statistic's properties (Douglas, 1987).

However, under very general circumstances, we know what the sampling distributions of the slope parameters of such a model are, and, although we might not care about these in our simulation, we can use this theoretical knowledge to check whether our simulation is performing as desired. Another trick is to run the simulation with no random error in the model and check whether the exact pseudo-population parameter values are estimated from a pseudo-sample.

Once these natural segments of commands appear to be working as desired, link them together into a single experimental run of the whole simulation. Because the simulation is likely to be quite complex by this time, it is best during the debugging phase to run it with only a limited number of trials, say 10-50 instead of 1,000-10,000, to save time. When it appears to be running properly, increase the number of trials, keeping an eye on the results. Finally, once a program has been developed satisfactorily for a single experiment, you can embed it into a multiexperiment looping algorithm. Again, you should start with a limited number of experiments and a limited number of trials per experiment to save debugging time. A crucial point to check at this stage is how the pseudo-population parameters are incrementing between experiments and whether the results of these changes are what you desire. For example, if you increase the error weight on a regression model with each experiment, what is the effect on R^2 over many experiments? Nonlinear relationships among parameters and output, as between R^2 and error term size, are especially tricky here. As error increases, R^2 will decrease quickly first and then fall more slowly as it approaches its natural limit of .00. Often this sort of behavior needs to be assessed and addressed on a trial-and-error basis.

The process of developing a successful Monte Carlo simulation experiment program therefore is one of building slowly, piece by piece, until the entire structure is in place. If you write out the entire code for a complex simulation and run it from scratch, two things will happen. First, you will have both program errors and mistakes in the values returned (once you get the program to run completely through). This is inevitable, as every person who ever booted up a personal computer knows. Second, and more important, you will find it difficult to track down your mistakes. Although debugging the program using the error messages of your statistical software may allow you to arrive at some output eventually (maybe), you may not be able to figure out why, for example, your coefficient estimate is 10,000 times larger than you expected. It is hard to pinpoint multiple small errors working interactively deep in a complex program. At this point, you will likely decide to do what you should have done at the outset—work through the program small piece by small piece until the desired output is achieved.

Overall, although Monte Carlo simulation can require lots of programming and careful thinking, its potential benefits for the social sciences are great. Through it, social scientists will be able to extend and test the relatively narrow limits of classical parametric inference methods. This will allow for the more accurate statistical modeling of, and the deeper substantive understanding of, social phenomena.

NOTES

1. One exception to this is STATA, which included a Monte Carlo procedure from release 3.1. Many statisticians use S-PLUS, usually in conjunction with FORTRAN, for this sort of computer intensive work (Efron & Tibshirani, 1993, Appendix).

2. Lewis and Payne (1973) report a generating procedure that has a period of (2^{98} − 1) and is not dependent on word size.

3. Even when $G(\alpha)$ does not exist in closed form for a distribution function, it sometimes can be approximated using optimization techniques, as in Baird (1995).

4. Note that the natural log of y is taken in these commands instead of $1 - y$, as in the inverse distribution function in Table 2.1. This is done to streamline the command and is equivalent to the full version given that $1 - U(0, 1) \sim U(0, 1)$.

5. In a sense, all inverse transformation methods are composition methods in that each transforms a $U(0, 1)$ variable. For pedagogical purposes and to follow convention, I have distinguished these approaches.

6. These procedures generally use the Box-Mueller method (Box & Mueller, 1958) of combining two $U(0, 1)$ variables or the modified polar method of Marsaglia and Bray (1964).

7. Because of its relationship with the normal distribution, the lognormal distribution sometimes is described in terms of the characteristics of the normal variable from which it is derived, such as $L(\mu, \sigma^2)$. Care must be taken to determine which notation an author is using in a given context.

8. However, unless there is strong theoretical reason to do so, such as evaluating a procedure that makes these modeling errors, it is best to model a process as completely as possible in a Monte Carlo simulation.

9. The "enveloping" approach of Schmeiser and Shalaby (1980) referred to subsequently is another way in which to deal with distributions having infinite tails.

10. The PDF of the beta contains a scalar from the beta function in the denominator, which standardizes the numerator so that the PDF integrates to 1. GAUSS does not automatically return a beta function, but it does return a gamma function, which is related to the beta function as follows:

$$\text{Beta}(a, b) = \frac{\Gamma(a)\Gamma(b)}{\Gamma(a + b)}$$

where a and b are the parameters of the beta distribution to be generated.

11. When a and/or b is (are) less than 1, the modal value is undefined for $\text{Bet}(a, b)$ because the PDF asymptotically approaches the vertical axis at its upper and/or lower bound in these cases. Therefore, a peak density value needs to be set at some practical level. In the code displayed subsequently, I use a peak density value of 4.0.

12. This algorithm is derived from Rubinstein (1981, pp. 95-101).

13. Another way in which to think of the negative binomial distribution is that it is the distribution of the number of trials, x, until the fth failure of a binomial process with probability p of success.

98

14. Generalizability always is a major concern in experimental research, whether the experiment is a physical or mathematical one (Cook & Campbell, 1979, pp. 70-74).

15. This is a version of the estimator that King and Browning (1987) justified using asymptotic maximum likelihood arguments. Therefore, Monte Carlo experiments still need to be used to understand its behavior in finite samples.

16. Although Type I and II inferential errors usually are discussed in terms of hypothesis tests, their application to confidence intervals is straightforward.

17. I used residuals resampling bootstrapping (Mooney & Duval, 1993, pp. 16-17).

18. Only 1,000 trials were used in this experiment because of the computationally intensive nature of the bootstrap.

19. I thank Bob Duval for devising this neat trick.

20. There may be situations in which this distinction would be of interest, and an analysis of it would be a logical extension of the techniques in this section.

21. The absolute value of the error skew was used here, as skew direction was not a concern.

22. Using the same data not only reduces random error in the comparison but also speeds up the experiments as less data need to be generated (Ross, 1990, pp. 139-140).

REFERENCES

APTECH SYSTEMS, INC. (1994) *The GAUSS System Version 3.1.2.* Maple Valley, WA: Author.

BADGER, W. W. (1980) "An entropy-utility model for the size distribution of income." In B. J. West (Ed.), *Mathematical Models as a Tool for the Social Sciences.* New York: Gordon and Breach.

BAIRD, D. B. (1995) *PROBS.SRC: GAUSS Functions for the Normal, Student's t, Chi-Square, F, Poisson, Binomial, Negative Binomial and Gamma Distributions.* Lincoln, New Zealand: AgResearch.

BARTELS, L. M. (1993) "Messages received: The political impact of media exposure." *American Political Science Review, 87,* 267-285.

BECK, N., & KATZ, J. N. (1995) "What to do (and not to do) with time-series-cross-section data in comparative politics." *American Political Science Review, 89,* 634-647.

BOX, G. E. P., & DRAPER, N. R. (1987) *Empirical Model-Building and Response Surfaces.* New York: John Wiley.

BOX, G. E. P., & MUELLER, M. E. (1958) "A note on the generation of random normal deviates." *Annals of Mathematical Statistics, 29,* 610-611.

CICCHITELLI, G. (1989) "On the robustness of the one-sample *t*-test." *Journal of Statistical Computation and Simulation, 32,* 249-258.

COOK, T. D., & CAMPBELL, D. T. (1979). *Quasi-Experimentation.* Boston: Houghton Mifflin.

CROWELL, F. (1977) *Measuring Inequality.* Oxford, England: Philip Alan.

DAVIDSON, R., & MACKINNON, J. G. (1993) *Estimation and Inference in Econometrics.* New York: Oxford University Press.

DOUGLAS, S. M. (1987) *Improving the Estimation of a Switching Regressions Model: An Analysis of Problems and Improvements Using the Bootstrap.* Unpublished Ph.D. dissertation, University of North Carolina, Chapel Hill.

DUVAL, R. D., & GROENEVELD, L. (1987) "Hidden policies and hypothesis tests: The implications of Type II errors for environmental regulation." *American Journal of Political Science, 31,* 423-447.

EFRON, B. (1987) "Better bootstrap confidence intervals" (with discussion). *Journal of the American Statistical Association, 82,* 171-200.

EFRON, B., & TIBSHIRANI, R. J. (1993) *An Introduction to the Bootstrap.* London: Chapman & Hall.

EVANS, M., HASTINGS, N., & PEACOCK, B. (1993) *Statistical Distributions* (2nd ed.). New York: John Wiley.

EVERITT, B. S. (1979) "A Monte Carlo investigation of the robustness of Hotelling's one- and two-sample T^2 tests." *Journal of the American Statistical Association, 74,* 48-51.

EVERITT, B. S., & HAND, D. J. (1981) *Finite Mixture Distributions.* London: Chapman & Hall.

FISK, P. R. (1961) "The graduation of income distributions." *Econometrica, 29,* 171-185.

GADDUM, J. H. (1945) "Lognormal distributions." *Nature, 156,* 463-466.

GELMAN, A., CARLIN, J. B., STERN, H. S., & RUBIN, D. B. (1995) *Bayesian Data Analysis.* London: Chapman & Hall.

GHURYE, S. G. (1949) "On the use of Student's *t* test in an asymmetrical population." *Biometrika, 36,* 426-430.

GREENWOOD, M., & YULE, G. U. (1920) "An inquiry into the nature of frequency distributions representative of multiple happenings with particular reference to the occurrence of multiple attacks of disease or repeated accidents." *Journal of the Royal Statistical Society A, 83,* 255-279.

GROSECLOSE, T. (1994) "Testing committee composition hypotheses for the U.S. Congress." *Journal of Politics, 56,* 440-458.

HAIGHT, F. A. (1967) *Handbook of the Poisson Distribution.* New York: John Wiley.

HALL, P. (1992) *The Bootstrap and the Edgeworth Expansion.* New York: Springer-Verlag.

HAMMERSLEY, J. M., & HANDSCOMB, D. C. (1964) *Monte Carlo Methods.* London: Chapman & Hall.

HENDRY, D. F. (1984) "Monte Carlo experimentation in econometrics." In Z. Griliches and M. D. Intriligator (Eds.), *Handbook of Econometrics* (Vol. 2). Amsterdam, Netherlands: Elsevier.

HENDRY, D. F., & HARRISON, R. W. (1974) "Monte Carlo methodology and the finite sample behaviour of ordinary and two-stage least squares." *Journal of Econometrics, 2,* 151-174.

HOPE, A. C. A. (1968) "A simplified Monte Carlo significance test procedure." *Journal of the Royal Statistical Society B, 30,* 582-598.

JACKMAN, S. (1994) "Measuring electoral bias: Australia, 1949-1993." *British Journal of Political Science, 24,* 319-357.

JARQUE, C. M., & BERA, A. K. (1987) "A test for normality of observations and regression residuals." *International Statistical Review, 55,* 163-172.

JOHNSON, M. E. (1987) *Multivariate Statistical Simulation.* New York: John Wiley.

JOHNSON, N. L., & KOTZ, S. (1970a) *Continuous Univariate Distributions* (Vol. 1). New York: John Wiley.

JOHNSON, N. L., & KOTZ, S. (1970b) *Continuous Univariate Distributions* (Vol. 2). New York: John Wiley.

JOHNSON, N. L., KOTZ, S., & KEMP, A. W. (1992) *Univariate Discrete Distributions* (2nd ed.). New York: John Wiley.

KENDALL, M. G., & STUART, A. (1950) "The law of cubic proportions in election results." *British Journal of Sociology, 1,* 183-197.

KING, G. (1989) *Unifying Political Methodology.* New York: Cambridge University Press.

KING, G., & BROWNING, R. X. (1987) "Democratic representation and partisan bias in congressional elections." *American Political Science Review, 81,* 1251-1276.

KLEIJNEN, J. P. C. (1975) *Statistical Techniques in Simulation* (Vol. 2). New York: Marcel Dekker.

LEWIS, T. G., & PAYNE, W. H. (1973) "Generalized feedback shift register pseudo random number algorithm." *Journal of the Association of Computing Machinery, 20,* 456-468.

LIJPHART, A., & CREPAZ, M. M. L. (1991) "Corporatism and consensus democracy in eighteen countries: Conceptual and empirical linkages." *British Journal of Political Science, 21,* 235-246.

101

MACLAREN, M. D., & MARSAGLIA, G. (1965) "Uniform random number generators." *Journal of the Association of Computing Machinery, 12,* 83-89.

MARSAGLIA, G., & BRAY, T. A. (1964) "A convenient method for generating normal variables." *SIAM Review, 6,* 260-264.

MOHR, L. B. (1990) *Understanding Significance Testing* (Sage University Paper series on Quantitative Applications in the Social Sciences, series no. 07-073). Newbury Park, CA: Sage.

MOONEY, C. Z. (1995) "Conveying truth with the artificial: Using simulated data to teach statistics in the social sciences." *SocInfo Journal, 1,* 36-41.

MOONEY, C. Z. (1996) "Bootstrap statistical inference: Examples and evaluations for political science." *American Journal of Political Science, 40,* 570-602.

MOONEY, C. Z., & DUVAL, R. D. (1993) *Bootstrapping: A Nonparametric Approach to Statistical Inference* (Sage University Paper series on Quantitative Applications in the Social Sciences, series no. 07-095). Newbury Park, CA: Sage.

MOONEY, C. Z., & KRAUSE, G. (in press) "Of silicon and political science: Computationally intensive techniques of statistical estimation and inference." *British Journal of Political Science.*

PARKS, R. (1967) "Efficient estimation of a system of regression equations when disturbances are both serially and contemporaneously correlated." *Journal of the American Statistical Association, 62,* 500-509.

PLACKETT, R. L. (1958) "The principle of the arithmetic mean." *Biometrika, 45,* 130-135.

PLACKETT, R. L. (1972) "The discovery of the method of least squares." *Biometrika, 59,* 239-251.

RAND CORPORATION. (1955) *A Million Random Digits With 1,000,000 Normal Deviates.* Glencoe, IL: Free Press.

ROSS, S. M. (1990) *A Course in Simulation.* New York: Macmillan.

RUBINSTEIN, R. Y. (1981) *Simulation and the Monte Carlo Method.* New York: John Wiley.

SCHENKER, N. (1985) "Qualms about bootstrap confidence intervals." *Journal of the American Statistical Association, 80,* 360-361.

SCHMEISER, B. W., & SHALABY, M. A. (1980) "Acceptance/rejection methods for beta variate generation." *Journal of the American Statistical Association, 75,* 673-678.

SCHRODT, P. A. (1982) "A statistical study of the cube law in five electoral systems." *Political Methodology, 7,* 31-53.

SIMON, J. L., & BRUCE, P. (1991) "Resampling: A tool for everyday statistical work." *Chance, 4,* 22-32.

VON NEUMANN, J. (1951) "Various techniques used in connection with random digits." *Bureau of Standards Applied Mathematics Series, 12,* 36-38.

WHITE, H. (1980) "A heteroskedasticity-consistent covariance matrix and a direct test for heteroskedasticity." *Econometrica, 48,* 817-838.

ABOUT THE AUTHOR

CHRISTOPHER Z. MOONEY is Associate Professor of Political Science at West Virginia University. He received his Ph.D. in political science in 1990 from the University of Wisconsin–Madison. In addition to West Virginia University, he has taught American politics and research methods at the University of Wisconsin–Madison, University of Wisconsin–Milwaukee, and University of Essex (United Kingdom). Since 1994, he also has lectured at the Essex Summer School in Social Science Data Analysis and Collection. He has published widely in academic journals on U.S. state legislatures, public policy, and modern nonparametric inference techniques. He coauthored *Bootstrapping* (1993, Sage, with Robert D. Duval) and *West Virginia Politics and Government: Institutional Capacity and the Struggle for Responsible Government* (1996, with Richard A. Brisbin, Jr., Robert Jay Dilger, and Allan S. Hammock).

Quantitative Applications in the Social Sciences

A SAGE UNIVERSITY PAPER SERIES

$10.95 each

To order, please use order form on the next page.

Quantitative Applications in the Social Sciences

A SAGE UNIVERSITY PAPER SERIES

$10.95 each

Place
Stamp
here

SAGE PUBLICATIONS, INC.
P.O. BOX 5084
THOUSAND OAKS, CALIFORNIA 91359-9924